ADOLESCENCE
The Crises
of Adjustment

edited by
Simon Meyerson

Senior Psychologist, North Middlesex Hospital
Consultant Psychologist, Quaesitor, London

Foreword by Dr Robert Gosling

Senior Psychoanalyst, Consultant Psychiatrist, Chairman,
Professional Committee, Tavistock Clinic

London · George Allen & Unwin Ltd
Ruskin House · Museum Street

First Published in 1975

ISBN 0 04 150051 2 hardback
ISBN 0 04 150052 0 paperback

Printed in Great Britain
in 11/12 Times Roman type
by Willmer Brothers Limited, Birkenhead

ADOLESCENCE
The Crises
of Adjustment

Dedicated to
my mother, Mayasha
and my late father, Pinnie
who struggled with their many adolescent children
without the help of any experts.

FOREWORD

Everybody's head is set spinning when confronted by adolescence, the adolescent himself and his elders and youngers alike. For here is a young person caught up in a biological and social process, poised between childhood and becoming an adult, grappling with family life and with entanglements beyond the boundaries of his family. Everyone is involved. A new generation is emerging. The failings of the status quo are highlighted by the imminence of new solutions.

Within the political arena of his own family his childhood is never far away. It is present within himself in the patterns of response he has built up from powerful emotional experiences in his past, particularly experiences in his earliest years. It is also present to the extent that those about him are roughly the same people who took part in some of these determinative events and who therefore reinforce these patterns of response by contributing to a repetition of them. While such constancy will have played an important part in allowing the young person to develop some stability of personality, it is also bound to some extent to obstruct the development of new adaptations to new circumstances.

Just as the adolescent carries within him powerful residues from earlier family life, so too the parents have little alternative but to follow their own determinative experiences at the hands of their own families. Thus grandparents and great-grandparents and aunts and uncles may be having their say in the political arena even though they are not visibly present.

But beyond the arena of the family, what lies there? What is the alternative society, not only to the family as it is, but to

large-scale established society as well? In fact what lies
beyond is not only a powerful complex of relationships and
institutions, but also, particularly amongst peers, a nascent
society compounded of shared beliefs and hopes.

As the young person's perspicacity increases he is bound
to be confronted with the gap between his parents' personal
resources, their values and their perspectives on the one
hand, and the needs of the present on the other. Govern-
ments are never up to their tasks and are always working on
out-moded assumptions; this applies as much to the politics
of family life as to those of nations. In both cases, moreover,
a painful disparity appears between precept and performance. Parents who were once perceived as setting the pace
are now exposed as laggards who nevertheless are still in the
driver's seat. Developments of all kinds within society are
always rendering out-moded what the older generation can
bring to bear. Ingrained perspectives and developed skills
fail to encompass the changed circumstances. For some, for
example, this failure is brought home to them when con-
traception shifts from being a family option with moral over-
tones to being an ecological necessity all over the world; for
others it may be when a new chemical, such as cannabis,
arrives on a drug scene that felt fairly safe when dominated
by dear old alcohol. Much of the extra-familial arena is
therefore well beyond the regular expertise of parents and,
moreover, is as wide open to exploitation for personal ambition and commercial gain as it is to creativity. The search for
new ways of embodying ideals in new forms of adaptation is
as wide open to being trivialised into clichés of modishness
and rebellion as it is to being elaborated into real innovation.
There is no reason to suppose that the dynamics of the
alternative society will be any more benign than were the
politics of the family.

Perhaps the most pervasive influence on the adolescent
that both nourishes his development and threatens to make a
captive of him is the projection on to him by everyone,
including his peers, of hopes for the future. Ideals that have
languished are given a new stir of life when a new adult
appears. While this certainly provides him with the benefit of

a 'most favoured nation' policy, it also exposes him to bewildering and vicious attacks. For hopes that have come to nothing, ideals that have been betrayed, or more reflectively, visions you have not been able to sustain, all revive not only old glories but also old heart-breaks. In a domain where a lot of hearts have been broken, envy and vicious revenge are not far away. So the alternative society is not only suffused with everyone's hopes for a new world, it is also peppered with the envy and bitterness of those parts of us that have lost out. The adolescent scene is therefore populated by just as many unrealised dreams and ambitions and the debris of cruel fates as it is by the ghosts of parents, grandparents and the Fathers of Society.

In so far as we are focusing on such matters as how ideals are discovered to have been misplaced—and how, if they are not soon found other vehicles, hope languishes—we are focusing on a never ending process of development; a process of growth, decay and renewal. Why then is there a temptation to suppose that this process is a peculiarity of adolescence? It must be that with the emergence of physical maturity it is all given a new face both to those who thought the young person was a child and to the young person himself who is similarly surprised. It is a kind of 'first time', like the first time you fall in love. But then every time you fall in love is a unique experience and so is a 'first time'. This is a paradox that is better left as it is since any attempt to resolve it will turn trite. So perhaps adolescence is a paradigm of the 'the first time'—a revelation that we long for and fear.

In a field that extends so far in social and psychological space as well as in time it is hard to bring to bear an adequate perspective. At the moment, and maybe for some time to come, the best we can do is to have a continuous colloquium amongst colleagues keeping us alive to the various features of this dynamic field. To this end Simon Meyerson has drawn together a number of colleagues, many of them at the Tavistock Clinic, who are variously pre-occupied with intrapsychic conflicts, family dynamics and social processes in and between institutions. But more importantly, they are colleagues who are prepared to expose themselves to the uncertainties and the vigour of so-called adolescents, and then to make a considered statement about their experience. What is now needed by the reader is to get all the facets here presented into focus all at the same time, like seeing the totality of a well-cut precious stone. For a moment he might then be in a good position to help an adolescent, whether himself or another, to negotiate his unique and undefined course. It is as if he should run through all this book on one breath, like a sprinter. In fact, most of the contributions in this volume merit such detailed consideration that each one in turn pushes the others out of focus. So it will be a struggle for us to look at each piece in detail and then to reconstruct the whole. But the struggle is a worthwhile one, and if it is successful it will be the editor and his contributors that the reader has to thank.

Robert Gosling
Tavistock Clinic
April 1974

About the Authors

JOHN BYNG-HALL is Consultant Psychiatrist to the Department of Children and Parents, Tavistock Clinic and Camden Assessment Centre.

MARY CAPES is Honorary Consultant in Child and Adolescent Psychiatry to Wessex Regional Hospital Board. She was formerly Director of the Child Guidance Clinic at Southampton and Consultant to the Mental Health Section of WHO.

ELISABETH HENDERSON is a Senior Social Worker and Psychotherapist at the Tavistock Clinic.

SUSAN HOLLAND was a Senior Psychologist at the Tavistock Clinic until 1973, when she left to set up the Battersea People's Aid and Action Centre.

ARTHUR HYATT WILLIAMS is a Senior Psychoanalyst, a Consultant Psychiatrist and Chairman of the Adolescent Department, Tavistock Clinic. He is also visiting psychotherapist to Wormwood Scrubs.

JUDITH ISSROFF is a Consultant Psychiatrist and Psychoanalyst who specialised in child, adolescent and social psychiatry at the Tavistock Institute, where she now continues her work in family psychiatry and community health.

SIMON MEYERSON is Senior Psychologist at the North Middlesex Hospital and is a Group Therapist at Quaesitor, London. Previously he was Senior Psychologist at the Tavistock Institute and the Adolescent Department of the Tavistock Clinic.

MARILYN MILLER's career in social work has concentrated on adolescents and mental health. She has worked at Long Grove Adolescent Unit and Hill End and is now at the Tavistock Clinic.

PAUL UPSON is Senior Clinical Psychologist in the Adolescent Department of the Tavistock Clinic.

CONTENTS

1

The Early Years

A. HYATT WILLIAMS

As Freud pointed out nearly seventy years ago, most of the problems which arise in adolescence are really rooted in infancy and there is an interaction between constitutional endowment with its resultant array of proclivities on the one hand and the circumstances of life as they impinge on the individual on the other. What happens depends upon how the polarities of these interlinking influences can be resolved. The factors which influence development, whether intra-psychic or interpersonal, are a good deal more complicated than one can describe briefly. Only some of these factors will be traced.

In some ways the easiest to delineate are the invariable patterns which can be seen in everyone. For example, the human baby, requiring such a very long period of nurture, is unique in the animal kingdom. At the age at which most of the higher mammals are capable of separate survival and fending for themselves, the human being is still utterly dependent upon parental care. The young monkey and the young baby born on the same day respond to life's experiences in quite different ways. For a long time the young monkey is very much quicker to learn than the baby and races ahead of the baby in almost every field of endeavour. Chief of these is mobility. At the age of two years however, when the baby is far from entering its most intense learning years, the monkey slows down and the baby passes the anthropoid in almost every field except that of movement. At about the age of two, the monkey is reaching sexual maturity but the young baby is still negotiating the various phases of infantile sexuality, still dependent upon the care of adults. It seems that the onset of sexual maturity has a marked influence upon the halting, or at least slowing, of further learning potential. This may be relevant later when one comes to consider the way in which an all too early puberty is sometimes associated with a fizzling out of learning potentials.

The development of the young infant may be considered in several different ways. The standard psychoanalytic approach associated with the name of Freud involves the recognition of certain phases of emotional development beginning with the earliest phase, the oral, going on to the anal, the phallic and the infantile genital or Oedipal stage. Then in a more or less decisive way infantile sexuality undergoes a recession round about the fifth or sixth year and from then on until the first stirrings of puberty there occurs the so-called latency period. This period is very important because a great proportion of the young person's energy is devoted to social activities, learning activities and the task of acquiring poise and balance in the environment, beginning of course with the family and going on to the school and other groupings.

One of Freud's colleagues, Karl Abraham, divided the oral phase into two stages: the first associated with sucking (oral erotic), and the second when the milk-teeth begin to erupt, with biting (oral sadistic). This is quite meaningful because in terms of object relationships the sucking relationship is very different from the biting relationship to an object or a part-object. An object technically means a person who is the object of a form of relationship, e.g. sucking, biting, loving. The first object is the mother, but in the earliest phase of life she is perceived and experienced not as a whole object, the mother, but in part-object terms, namely the nipple, the breast and various other parts which are in one way or another related to the young infant and its needs. The young infant himself consists of an animated bundle of helplessness dominated by alimentary activities, tissue with vast potential surrounding a food tube. Need and greed can manifest themselves from the earliest phase of infancy onwards. When the milk-teeth erupt, direct pain can be inflicted upon the nipple and breast and of course other objects and part-objects can be attacked similarly. The way in which the teeth are used depends not only upon gratification and frustration of primary needs but also upon the infant's innate *quantum* of aggressiveness. The eruption of the milk-teeth is often associated with weaning, that is the loss of the primary object, the breast. Freud refers to this in a very meaningful way in the third of his three essays on sexuality. To quote Freud,

> 'on the psychical side the process of finding an object for which preparations have been made from earliest childhood is completed. At a time at which the first beginnings of sexual satisfaction are still linked with the taking of nourishment, the sexual instinct has a sexual object outside the infant's own body in the shape of his mother's breast. It is only later that the instinct loses that object, just at the time, perhaps, when the child is able to form a total idea of the person to whom the organ giving some satisfaction belongs. As a rule the sexual instinct then becomes auto-erotic and not until the period of latency has been passed through is the original relation restored. There are thus good reasons why a child sucking at his mother's breast has become the prototype of every relation of love. The finding of an object is in fact a refinding of it.'

The next phase of emotional development described by Freud was the anal phase, dominated by toilet training. The anal phase reverses the main feature of the oral phase in that instead of demands being made by the infant upon the mother, or her substitute, there is a situation in which she makes demands upon the infant and in which there are more or less strenuous efforts to control one aspect of his bodily and mental functioning. He is asked to part not only with something regarded by him as part of himself, but, at a time not of his own choosing. These experiences can easily make the infant feel persecuted by the demands. But the infant can easily wreak vengeance by frustrating the parent in refusing the demand. Freud described anal eroticism as the pleasure associated with both the retention of the faeces by the infant within himself and also the pleasure obtained from the expulsion of the bowel content, particularly when the infant does this from choice. Thus the anal phase is dominated by object-relatedness. The anal phase, as Freud described it, is characterised by a triad of traits, based on the wish to retain and the wish to expel. The faeces are felt to be a part of the infant at first and then to become not a part of him. This stage can have a marked effect on the later development of character. In a paper written in 1908 called 'Character and Anal Eroticism', Freud described how fixations at the anal stage can cause an emphasis on parsimony, that is the refusal to part with money, but also extending to other things like giving—derived from a reluctance and refusal to part with faeces. The second characteristic in the anal triad is cleanliness and this is a reaction formation against the wish to soil and dirty. The third characteristic is orderliness and in this the individual seems to take on the characteristics of the controlling parent in endeavouring to have everything just right and under his control.

Freud described the anal stage of development as the anal-sadistic stage because at this particular time in the relationships between parent and child, and the child and his own stools, the characteristics of self-assertion, of withholding and evacuating can usually be associated with a great deal of aggressiveness and cruelty which seems particularly to gather round these activities. This is not to contradict the fact that there is also cruelty derived from the oral phase. But there is a difference. Oral cruelty is a very much more frightening and devouring thing, particularly when one sees it in criminal acts like mugging, which involves robbery by violence. Anal cruelty can be seen also in relationship to obedience to controlling forces: sometimes they are the forces of law and order; sometimes the forces of more subversive organisations. Abraham, from his former speciality as an embryologist, again subdivided Freud's phases of emotional development into an anal retentive phase and an anal expulsive phase and stated and described how these two phases differ in the kind of object relations and the kind of phantasies which dominate at these particular times and influence later relationships.

Although Freud had drawn attention to the Oedipus complex in his book *The Interpretation of Dreams* published in 1900, he did not describe the phallic phase until 1923. During this next phase the little boy is dominated by conscious and unconscious feelings about his penis and concern for its safety. The little girl is concerned with the absence of a penis and resentful about her feeling of organ inferiority. This must be the earliest determining cause of recruitment to Women's Lib. The phallic phase in little boys can be characterised by proud, swashbuckling, daring, defiant behaviour. It has an exhibitionist flavour. There seems to be a denial of fear and anxiety although this denial often wears thin and the main anxiety is associated with the fear of loss of the penis experienced as castration anxiety. This is the phase at which little boys often play with matches and light fires, and also the time when there is often a recrudescence of nocturnal bed-wetting. The little girl, feeling castrated, develops penis envy and moves to the father as compensation. This phase merges into the infantile, genital or Oedipal phase, according to classical Freudian theory, from the age of three to five. In the Oedipus situation or the infantile genital organisation, the child develops a primarily loving and erotic attitude towards the parent of the opposite sex together with rivalry, jealousy and sometimes hostility towards the parent of the same sex. Thus little boys will tend to love their mothers and be in rivalry with, and sometimes fear, their fathers but they will also model themselves upon their fathers. Little girls will develop a primarily loving relationship with their fathers and develop rivalry, jealousy and hostility as well as identification with their mothers.

It will be seen that there is really a four-fold relationship in the Oedipus situation. The little boy has a libidinal link with the mother and a wish to be like his father, but at the

17

B

same time a tendency to develop a hostile relationship with him or with his internal image. In miniscule, however, the reverse situation holds good with a rivalry and hostile situation in relationship to mother and a libidinal link with father. This depends upon the extent to which the little boy has within himself a psychic organisation in which he either feels himself to be, or behaves as if he were, a little girl. Similarly, the little girl has a primarily libidinal link with father and a rivalling, primarily hostile relationship with mother. But the opposite is represented in miniscule exactly as in the case of the little boy. This consists of a loving libidinal link with mother and a hostile rivalry with father. It might be seen from these formulations, first clearly set out by Freud at the turn of the century, where homosexuality of a psychic kind originates. One can visualise situations in which the balance between male and female feelings runs counter to the ordinary biological direction and how sensitive and subtle identity difficulties can multiply.

But bisexuality is part of our human endowment so that however strong the emphasis is upon the heterosexual link and the development of heterosexual object relationships, there is always some representation of the homosexual link and some development of emotional but not acted out homosexual relationships. A good deal of the later difficulties in adolescence, for example, depend upon the decisiveness of these steps towards sexual identity which are taken when the child is under the sway of the infantile genital organisation.

Reference has already been made to the latency period— that period of apparent quiescence and righteous social imitation which follows in the wake of the massive repression of the Oedipus complex. This comparatively conflict-free period of latency is broken by the stirrings of puberty (see next chapter).

During childhood there are many other factors at work. There is the growing complexity of the relationship between the child, mother and father and other siblings who precede or succeed him.

There are subtler rivalries based upon such factors as position in the family: what the immediately older sibling was like, how the individual was treated by this particular sibling, what the immediate younger sibling was like and what the others were like. The only child has a psychodynamic make-up of his own and so does the eldest child, the youngest child as well as the second child.

Level of intelligence is, of course, important. Within the social environment, particularly the family environment, a child who is vastly lower in intelligence from the rest of the family, or vastly higher, is likely to be to some extent maladapted. Of course frequently, but not necessarily, the one that is higher in intelligence has a far better chance of adjusting at home or finding a satisfactory peer group. Also intelligence does seem to give a person an instrument of retrospective examination, a review of what has gone on and a capacity to learn from experience so that future happenings can to some extent be guided. Incidentally, the conscious direction of life can be effective only to a very limited extent. Various difficulties are inevitable and a number of difficulties which are not inevitable do arise by contingency. Some of these are very important, such as early separation from the mother or her surrogate which was first described by Bowlby and then elaborated in convincing detail with full visual evidence by the Robertsons. Separations between the ages of six months and three years are very important in future character development and personality integration. Most very disturbed adolescents, such as severe delinquents, seem to have had some early experiences of loss which they have been unable to work through. As has been stated by Sir Keith Joseph, in his address to the Playgroups Association, 'the cycle of deprivation' tends to be worse when the social environment, the family history and the personalities of the immediate forebears, together with the possibility of genetic factors, conspire together to reinforce an already bad situation. If, to this already worsened situation, there are further contingencies such as separation, severe painful illness, cruelty or sexual seduction, it will be seen how indelible the experiences can be and how the best endeavours of the remedial services can be frustrated. In minor degree, of course, separation which is not worked through is exceedingly common, the more so since the Second World War when most mothers of young children do go out to work. Of course, it varies considerably with the length of time the child is left and the way in which the mother compensates. Most important, of course, is the way the particular child can adapt to frustration and can sustain some kind of contact with the absent mother by retaining an introjected image of the loved mother during the periods when she is away for long periods.

One of the measures which looked as though it was a thoroughly good thing at the time and which turned out to be disastrous when viewed in retrospect was the wartime evacuation and separation of children from their parents. Not only was there a great deal of separation and deprivation as far as human relationships were concerned, but there was also a loss of geographical and temporal security and social displacement added to the strain so that the children became disturbed partly by their natures and partly because they had to leave their mothers at a crucial time of anxiety, as well as being called upon to adjust sometimes to an altogether different social environment. No wonder they became ill-adapted and part of their maladaptation was regarded by the people upon whom they were billeted as typical of their district, social class or way of life. Alienation, of course, took place at this point and tended to get worse. Once established, this is very difficult to remedy, and for many years after the war one saw what an effect evacuation continued to have upon individual development.

Traumatic incidents, whether involving a threat to life, castration threat, or exciting events such as seduction of various kinds, can produce far-reaching effects upon the development of the character and personality. Before 1897 Freud thought that all hysterics had been actually seduced.

I wish to turn to one of the concepts which I have found useful in understanding early development. It is Bion's concept of the container and the contained. It would seem that in the early phases of infantile development the infant is a totally inadequate container for the powerful unorganised impulses of which he is the owner. One of the main functions

20

of the mother or her surrogate is to act as a container so that some of the difficulties can be relayed to her. She can be filled with them and then, if she is a good mother or mother surrogate, she is able in some way to hold, mull over and improve to some extent, so that what she relays back to the young child has been rendered somewhat more psychically acceptable and the infant is now more able to cope with those elements. If the infant or young child is endowed with extremely strong impulses or somewhat distorted ones and the parent or surrogate is not able to contain the various direct or indirect communications, this favourable trans-action of having the communication improved, relayed back in a form more capable of being worked upon and within the infant's capacity does not take place. That is, the mother does not know how to emotionally help her child. Sometimes there is simply no response from the mother and the infant can rightly feel misunderstood by not being contained. In other cases, where the mother, for example, is either a schizoid person herself or the so-called schizophrenogenic mother, the communications may be so horrific to the mother that she strips them of all meaning, distorts them and feeds them back to the infant in a much worse state than they were in when they came to her. Thus, what could be a communication with the possibility of growth and develop-ment becomes a communication which blights and distorts the development of the infant or young child. It is sometimes in these circumstances that delinquency can be regarded, as Winnicott regarded it, as a surge of optimism following a period of hopelessness. In stealing in particular, or acquisit-ive delinquency in general, there is some idea that something good exists, that he can get hold of it, but because of old patterns of disappointment and hopelessness, he feels he is in some way justified to try to take it by storm.

The concept of the container and the contained is useful for it applies throughout development. Where this relation-ship is inappropriate between the two persons or the adoles-cent and his parent or environment, normal development falters and disturbance and acting-out occurs, partly because of the upset of the balance and partly to find some balance.

At this point I will move to the post-Freudian views of Melanie Klein on early emotional development. Her views supplement and extend but do not contradict Freud's findings. In 1920 Freud finally abandoned his view that there were not two separate instincts, a sexual one and an aggressive one. In his classic paper 'Beyond the Pleasure Principle', he delineated two main instincts which determine human activity. One is the life instinct, which includes instinctual organisations and impulses, and the other is the death instinct, which expresses a constitutional built-in trend towards the limitation of life, finally terminating in the extinguishing of life. Following on from *Beyond the Pleasure Principle* Freud, in 1923, wrote another important monograph, *The Ego and the Id*, in which he reformulated his theory of instincts and delineated a structure of the personality into ego, superego and id. Melanie Klein started off by fully accepting Freud's theory of life and death instincts and the ultimate polarity of these two opposing currents in determining our human behaviour. She also stated that the important psychic mechanisms of projection and introjection begin from the moment of birth and, in fact, recent unpublished work indicates that there is some evidence of psychic life before birth (although Melanie Klein does not say so). By the mechanism of projection the infant is able to explore the environment, including all the people in it and particularly those closest to him. The repeated interchanges of projection and introjection, reprojection and reintrojection cause a gradual build-up of the ego of the infant.

In the earliest phases there is no concept of a whole person but rather a perception of parts of persons. For example, mother is perceived as a nipple or a breast, as touching hands, engulfing arms and so on. In the earliest phase of life the dominant kind of anxiety present in the infant is what Melanie Klein calls persecutory anxiety. All approaches to the infant are designated as hostile and persecutory until they are proved otherwise. During this early phase and owing to the built-in tendency of the mother to care for and cherish young infants, the infant experiences the caring, feeding mother as a good feeding breast, and she gradually becomes delineated from unpleasant persecutory experiences. So two sets of experiences begin to be codified: that which is not wanted or the absence of that which is wanted. On the one hand the gratifying experience is supposed to derive from the good object, and the bad experiences derived from the bad object—both still perceived in part-object terms. This early differentiation into good, gratifying experiences coming from a good, gratifying breast, and bad, persecutory experiences stemming from a bad, persecutory breast are very important. Those individuals who are unable to separate the good from the bad breast seem to be vulnerable to later confusion and persecutory feelings. With the re-emergence of infantile feeling at adolescence, good and bad get mixed up together. We see the end product of this muddle of good and bad parts clinically in some of the more disturbed and disintegrated adolescents.

Melanie Klein described how the anxieties of a persecutory type reach a kind of zenith or climax at about the end of three months or so after birth, lasting over a few weeks or months. She labelled this somewhat extended period of time the paranoid schizoid position. Paranoid, because the predominant kind of anxiety is persecutory and schizoid because fixations at this early stage are associated with later tendencies to break down into schizophrenic kinds of illness.

At about the age of five or six months, because of growth and more integrated perceptive apparatus, together with a certain amount of psychic maturation, the infant becomes able to perceive and experience his mother not only as nipple, breast and hands (part-objects) in a conglomerate, but as a person (a whole object at last). This moment of integration and wholeness first of all is maintained for moments only before the persecutory anxiety, of tenuous, struggling, threateningly dependent existence again supervenes. However, with increasing development and in favourable circumstances, there are more and more extensions of the time during which the infant experiences the mother as a whole person. This poses the infant with problems, because the earliest splitting out into good, gratifying, and bad, persecuting part-objects becomes no longer fully

23

possible when the infant perceives that the mother is the very same person from whom both kinds of experience stem. At this moment the infant becomes afraid that his feelings of hostility directed against the bad, depriving, frustrating breast will also destroy the good, gratifying and love-giving breast now that he has found and realised that both aspects belong to one mother. There is therefore concern, guilt, remorse, depression, sadness lest the harm done by hatred should damage or destroy or drive away the good object and that the love and reparation will not be able to offset or mitigate the bad, destructive feelings. This phase, which is not accomplished in a day or two but which goes on for quite a long time, Melanie Klein called the depressive position. The successful negotiation of this phase is regarded as central to later happiness, love, creativity and the capacity to care, experience and radiate goodness—as well as to becoming a 'good', emotionally healthy person.

If the outcome of the depressive position is favourable integration and non-persecutory, whole-object relationships tend to predominate from then on. Following in the wake of the negotiation of the depressive position, there is a marked reduction of both persecutory and depressive anxiety; the way is left open for further growth and development of the infant, the capacity for sublimation increases, and the learning processes are facilitated. Nobody negotiates the depressive position so perfectly that there is no further recrudescence of persecutory anxiety. The situation or position can be regarded as being more or less negotiated. In the face of mounting external or internal stress, there tends to be a relapse back into disintegration of whole-object relationships and into a state dominated once again by persecutory anxiety. Most of us throughout life move up and down this scale or spectrum. There seems a parallel between a successful negotiation of the depressive position or a successful renegotiation of it and what the religious teachers would term a state of grace. The opposite is a state leading to breakdown or antisocial behaviour, dominated by feelings of persecution, irritability, resentfulness, desire for revenge and so on. At this point it may be that the polarities between depressive and persecutory anxiety are too great to be integrated and an ego splitting takes place so that the individual subsequently behaves as if he or she were in fact two or more persons. One sees some Dr Jekyll and Mr Hyde situations, particularly in delinquents, where the Dr Jekyll part is dominated by depressive anxiety and the Mr Hyde part riven by persecutory anxiety. Some young adolescents opt out of both kinds of anxiety or can go from an ill-negotiated sortie into the depressive position, where they care for the whole world's problems, back down the spectrum into persecutory anxiety, opting out of all feelings or relationships with other people into a global state of not caring. Often, at this point, young people seek a peer group in order to share an emotionally supercharged and highly unsatisfactory situation. If the young person is sufficiently integrated to overcome persecutory anxiety he is more likely to join groups whose preoccupation is not to project persecution outwards into others. The person who is able, in infancy, to make some satisfactory negotiation of the depressive position, it will be seen, is in a far better state for further development and for coping with the internal feelings of adolescence as well as environmental hazards of all kinds.

Most of the hurdles, landmarks or possible fixation points of human development are not entirely negotiated, nor usually is there an entire failure to negotiate them. As was mentioned earlier, referring to the way in which the depressive position is partly negotiated, so also are the main phases partly negotiated—the oral phase, the anal phase, the phallic and Oedipal phases of emotional development. For normal development, a lot depends upon the quantitative factor, the degree to which these positions and phases have been negotiated. Sometimes when merely an apparent negotiation has taken place the personality may appear stable. But if there is not sufficient resolution of the infantile conflicts integrated into the personality, when new difficulties are encountered or particularly when a series of traumatic situations assail the individual too quickly, before adequate time for working through can be obtained, those outposts or highlights of early development which are flimsily held are

25

abandoned and there is a movement regressively to a stage of emotional development which is more firmly held. What we are now describing is regression. At this point it has been described in some detail because it makes clear and understandable such happenings as the child who does very well up to a given point and then at a given juncture, usually about puberty, there seems to be a catastrophe so that he goes to pieces and the bright promise disappears. Hopefully, these disturbances can, if the environment is containing in an understanding way, be worked through. Just as a reunited fractured limb may be strongest where the fracture once was, so the healed traumatised area of the mind may become stronger once working through and healing have taken place.

2

Puberty and Phases of Adolescence

A. HYATT WILLIAMS

The process of adolescence is a normal phenomenon which takes what seems a long and yet a short period of time. In this process there are both risks and opportunities. There is, as Freud stated in 1905, a rapid recapitulation of earlier phases of emotional development. In addition there are the special tasks of puberty (see later) and also various complicated problems like education, relations to peer groups, leisure and ambition.

Because so much is happening so quickly, it will be seen that certain stresses may be more than the individual can bear even though until puberty he had developed apparently normally. There can be a failure to cope, leading to a dropping out or to an actual emotional or psychic breakdown. In addition to this kind of fresh failure is the failure which was laid down previously at one or many fixation points during early emotional development in infancy and childhood which was not discernible during the latency period, so that it remained relatively unseen. The exacerbation in a dangerous way occurs when the adaptive resources of the young person are taxed beyond their limit during adolescence.

A great deal depends upon the cultural environment in which puberty and adolescence are taking place. Partly because of our western European family structure and also other social structures, puberty and adolescence have been regarded and still are looked upon as particularly stressful both to the individual who is involved with them and to the adults of various kinds such as parents, teachers and so on, who are involved in trying to respond to the varied demands and needs of the adolescent. Often, in rebellion against and alienation from the social climate of the time, that is the world of adults, the adolescent acting within a peer group seeks or finds himself involved in a subculture or counter-culture. In so far as this involves a fresh thinking out of old problems and a new approach, it may be a progressive and essential phenomenon which occurs with each generation. On the other hand, depending upon the violence and hatred involved in the rejection of parents, parental figures, authorities and their representatives, there is often, as well as a rejection of the confused and possibly hypocritical attitudes of the older generation, a rejection of the creative, tolerant and constructive attitudes which are progressive or forma-tive. The capacity to grow towards freedom depends upon the constructive use of past experiences, including those dur-ing early life with the parents and with the family social constellation.

To distinguish between the term puberty and adolescence: puberty is a term which describes the inevitable, physical, endocrine and physiological changes which take place when the latency child starts to grow and to mature sexually. By this is really meant biological sexuality. Adolescence refers to a process of emotional development and attempts at adaptation to the new situation with which the young person is confronted by the changes intrinsic in having reached puberty. The reactions, the emotions, the social behaviour etc. of young people may have been detonated by the biologi-cal event of puberty but the whole process of adaptation constitutes the adolescent process and it ends with the stabilisation and slowing or halting of the psychic and emotional ferment. At this point the young person has become an adult. When the young person presents himself for treatment of emotional problems, these different aspects of puberty and adolescence appear in a very confused pattern from which the various components have to be sorted out.

In our culture, as was stated, the impact of puberty results in the turbulence of adolescence. The way in which the young person handles this depends on his capacity, upon circumstances including his social environment, upon chance happenings such as health, brief or prolonged physical illness, academic success or failure which might itself result in his being moved or moving to quite a different social environment and his response to the cultural impact of that milieu. For example, when a bright young man from a working-class home is accepted for Oxford or Cambridge, goes to live away from his home and meets a group of very bright people, altogether unexpected stresses and rewards are to be found.

It is important to remember that the invariables to do with puberty and adolescence still operate, although the way in which problems are worked out varies very widely from generation to generation of adolescents. The false solutions, crime, drug-taking and escaping into easy options, look new but are all old ways in which psychic pain can be avoided. In the present generation of adolescents, it is the way of working out the problem which has changed.

Phases of Adolescence

Derek Miller described early and middle and late adolescence and said that the three phases were distinguishable from each other.

In an attempt to summarise Miller's views, it would appear that early adolescence is characterised by the plea for help from parents and other authorities in an attempt to control the strange urges and rumblings which are going on inside the early adolescent who, though well adapted to childhood, is as yet quite unadapted to the changes in himself which are going on.

Middle adolescence is characterised by the plea to be left alone and to develop in his or her own way. It is this total change in the need situation that makes the problem for the parents quite difficult because the child who, a short while earlier, had made most demands for help has now undergone a *volte-face* and is striving and demanding to be left alone. It depends upon the way in which both parents and adolescents relate and cope with each other in this phase whether the turning away is able to proceed relatively smoothly or whether there is a great deal of emotional wounding by parents and frantic, fugitive behaviour on the part of the adolescent.

Late adolescence is characterised by considerable rivalry with parents. The adolescent has now a certain arrogance in that the parents are usually designated as 'past it' or 'has beens', and it is quite clear that the late adolescent exaggerates the fact that the future belongs to him or her and not to the parents. A lot depends upon the way in which the turning away from the parents is carried out, in particular whether it is with reasonable tolerance or with massive hatred and rejection. The parents influence the course of the development of the late adolescent in that they can acquiesce, or be indifferent or can be unduly punitive. Sometimes, in confusion, they can inconsistently try all these methods. In other words, during adolescence there is a very lively interaction between parents and adolescent and much depends upon the way in which parents and adolescents can learn from the experience of this interaction.

Emotional Development at Adolescence

As was stated in the initial paragraph of this chapter, there is a reactivation in the young adolescent of the emotional and psychosocial development which was temporarily broken off at the age of five or six with what Freud called 'the dissolution of the Oedipus complex, resulting in the latency period'. At adolescence, however, sexual thoughts, fantasies and impulses are backed by powerful chemical driving forces. The unresolved Oedipal situation froths to the surface again. The earlier stages of emotional development—the oral, the anal and the phallic phases—are run through in rapid succession with a speed almost like the rewinding of a cinematograph tape. These various repetitions of infantile experience are tried out, first with the parents or their surrogates. Later on they are tried out in new relationships. At some variable time in early adolescence or towards the second phase of adolescence, there is a turning towards a peer group, especially in boys.

The importance of the role played by unconscious factors cannot be overstressed. There is conflict between conscious thoughts and unconscious impulses. The driving power of the impulses is of instinctual origin, partly mentally and partly chemically fuelled.

In the third of his three essays on sexuality, Freud delineated the tasks of puberty as:

1. the crystallisation of sexual identity;
2. the finding of a sexual object; and
3. the bringing together of the two main stems of sexuality, namely the sensual one and the tender one.

In Freud's day, though not perhaps so much in contemporary society, the adolescent girl behaved in a somewhat different manner psychically from the adolescent boy. She had an extra task which was to alter her main pregenital orientation which was dominated by penis envy to that of true receptive femininity. Her primary erotogenic zone had to shift from the clitoris to the vagina before she could reach a fully female libidinal position. The work of Masters and Johnson throws some doubt upon this change of zone from a physical but not from a psychical viewpoint.

Confusions of sexual identity seem to be more common now than they were in Freud's time. Miller stated that if an adolescent is sure of his or her sexual identity the adolescent process proceeds relatively smoothly. Up to a point this is true, but it does not take into consideration many other factors, for example the strength of instinctual impulses, the quality of ego development, the way in which the ego can act as a framework to contain powerful instinctual urges without being disrupted and fragmented by their activities, and also it does not take into consideration the balance between aggressive and loving impulses. In any event, secure sexual

31

identity is the epilogue of adolescence, not its prologue.

One can look at the problem of development at puberty from a number of viewpoints. The one described is based rather on instincts and their gratification than upon object relationships. The whole problem can be studied from an object relationship viewpoint and their development during adolescence follows the same general rule that there is always a tendency to repeat the pattern of earlier relationships. Object relations have an intrapsychic and an interpersonal component.

Man appears to be unique in having an inner world which acts as a sort of harbour or sanctuary and which facilitates the use of fantasy in a series of pilot experiments so that the feel of a line of action and its probable consequences can be tried out and tested without anything irrevocable having been done in the external world. In some people, fantasy is used only as a precursor or a prelude to action. In others, it is used as a substitute for action. Most desirably, however, it is used as a reality test and in the case of unacceptable activities it may also give a token gratification which acts as a substitute for the actual deed.

Freud laid emphasis upon the fact that in adolescence both fantasy life and masturbation are greatly intensified. Adolescents who are able to use fantasy freely in the course and service of development are in a very much better position than those in whom fantasies are distorted or inhibited or act merely as a prelude to action. This last group, of course, contains delinquents and criminals. On the other hand the more schizoid adolescent may use fantasy as so much of a substitute for action and in the world of reality-testing and external life that he is completely without activity and seems to be without resources.

In one way adolescence itself is a pilot experiment in independent living. Adolescence provides another opportunity of working through the depressive position. If the anxieties to do with the depressive position are negotiated better in adolescence than they were in the original experience during the first year of life, there can be a marked acceleration of development and progress and this is sometimes seen educationally where the slow starter comes into the competition and outstrips his formerly more successful adversaries. If the depressive position is not negotiated as well in adolescence as it was in the original experience in the first year of life, there may be a much greater bogging down in a state of persecutory anxiety and the inner psychic life of the adolescent may become impoverished rather than enriched so that the psychosocial field may become a ground for the acting out of very disturbed feelings, theories and suppositions. It is this kind of adolescent who, since childhood, perhaps has lost through death or separation one or both parents, thus losing a vital part of the holding framework and cross-latticed matrix of family life. In this way a situation which was relatively satisfactory in early infancy has really changed very much for the worse during the phase of greatest need, namely the turmoil of adolescence. It is very common for the adolescent with both parents to become disillusioned with them as well as teachers and other adults and to turn to a group of his own contemporaries.

If no major fixations have been laid down at the earliest stages of emotional development of the first five years of life, and if the infantile depressive position has to some extent been negotiated, developmental progress during adolescence is likely to proceed with only a manageable amount of distress. If on the other hand there are major fixations, particularly in a psychosexual field, these are likely to be thrown into prominence and thereafter may become permanent features of the total personality and life of the individual.

There is a great increase in masturbation at puberty. This was emphasised by Freud in the third of the *Three Essays on the Theory of Sexuality*. He stressed how the frequency of masturbation had declined markedly with the onset of the latency period. Masturbation, however, is very complicated with conscious fantasies associated with it, and beneath these, of course, are unconscious fantasies and impulses. Sometimes masturbation with aggressive or perverse fantasies provides a pilot experiment, useful because it can take place without committing its practitioner to all the other

33

side-effects of acting out socially unacceptable aggressive or perverse sexual fantasies. Sometimes, however, there is a settling down to masturbation as an end in itself and this is usually in narcissistic individuals so that masturbation is not used as a bridge to a more balanced and developed kind of sexual fantasy or relationship. Sometimes there is a split in the sexuality of the individual, which becomes manifest at puberty and then becomes entrenched for the rest of the sexual life of the individual. In this condition there is a relatively normal sexuality as well as perverse, sadistic, sado-masochistic or even murderous sexuality expressed in fantasies associated with masturbation. Sometimes masturbatic fantasies consist of robbing and destroying the sexual object and sometimes of evacuating badness identified with urine and faeces into it.

There is much more freedom in the attitudes to behaviour in general and in particular sexuality is a great deal freer between adolescents than it has been for the past century. Sometimes in this climate of freedom to enjoy normal sexuality is posed the problem about what to do with bad or perverse sexuality viewed by the individual as entirely unacceptable in relationship to any sexual object. Traditionally and over many centuries, the bad aspects of sexuality of men were in some way mitigated by relationships with prostitutes. Prostitutes could therefore be viewed as people who were able to localise and contain some sexual disturbance of men and who by their often ill-appreciated behaviour saved society from more widely scattered perverse sexual ravages.

When the adolescent chooses a partner who in some way takes over from, or is in the idiom of the person who formerly helped, fed, clothed and protected the individual, Freud termed it an anaclytic object choice. If the choice is a narcissistic one the love object is chosen in the individual's own image and represents himself. I think part of what was traditionally described as the pining and wasting away as seen in some young people who fall in love is due to the challenge and competition of the love of another person with the self-love of the individual. In the narcissistic kind of object choice one finds that there is a history of a violent rejection of the primal object, mother or her substitute, often in the face of the first great stress period, namely weaning. The individual then turns to himself and withdraws his emotional investment from mother or her substitute and invests himself with all the feeling, including especially the eroticisation. He therefore goes through a secondary narcissistic phase from which he usually does not recover. When later he chooses a partner, if that partner is in his own image, standing for himself, it can be seen that the relationship is far more tyrannical, demanding, inflexible and rigid than in the case of the anaclytic kind of object choice. It is for this reason that narcissistic choices of partner have a much worse prognosis either in general relationships or subsequently in marriage than the anaclytic choices. The person with the narcissistic kind of object relationship is more brittle and vulnerable and is more liable to break down personally, or the relationship is more likely to break down because it does not really involve emotional sharing with another; rather narcissism, deep down, is an act of isolation.

It has been stated that often new relationships which develop in adolescence follow in the groove of the old relationships which pervaded childhood and infancy and repeat the old pattern. There is another way of responding, namely the substitution of the reverse and choosing a partner who is least like the mother or her substitute, or in the case of the girl, the boy who is least like the father or his substitute. The degree of hatred involved in the renunciation of the primary object determines whether the choice of the secondary object is likely to be stably based or not. Interestingly, the girl having chosen a partner who is exactly the opposite in every way to her father may find later on in life that the very relationship she yearns for most is a relationship with a man like her father, and at that point unless a lot of good work has gone on from a developmental viewpoint, her marriage is likely to break down.

In 1910–12 Freud wrote three short papers on the psychology of love. The first was entitled 'A Common Cause of

Debasement in the Field of Love' and this is to do with the tendency towards the non-confluence of the two main currents of eroticism, namely the sacred and the profane, so that a man cannot lust where he loves, and he cannot love where he lusts. An example is Goldsmith's *She Stoops to Conquer*. The second of Freud's papers is entitled 'A Special Type of Object Choice Made by Men'. Here the woman has to be unavailable, not his, married to someone else, possibly of rather notorious reputation and so on. Sometimes the state of conflict is projected into the love object, who is seen to be fascinating and frightening. The frightening, seductive, formidable women found in some poems—Coleridge's 'Christabelle' or Keats's 'La Belle Dame Sans Merci'—are examples of this. This, of course, is a derivative of the young man's Oedipal love for his mother, displaced or projected on to somebody else who thus is coloured by his earlier experiences of his mother or who is sought in the image of the kind of mother that he has wished for. The third of the papers on the psychology of love is 'The Taboo of Virginity'. This deals with the fact that, although virginity was regarded as a highly desirable state for a girl to be in when she was chosen as a prospective wife, it was also very frightening. He referred to some cultures in which there was ritual defloration of the adolescent girl prior to her marriage so that the man who deflowered her was not required to spend his life with her. In this way the anger at her having been forced firmly into a castrated, penetrated, feminine position and reminded that she was not a man, that is not born with a penis, was felt towards a neutral religious or authority figure. One sees this kind of behaviour during the various courtship procedures and experiments of adolescents.

In a recent book entitled *Phallos*, Thorkil Vanguard has drawn attention to the way in which phallic aggression has become equated with masculinity and submissiveness with femininity. Submissiveness to phallic aggression by less strong men was regarded as the greatest of humiliations by people of certain cultures, notably the old Norse Vikings and some Arab societies in the Middle East.

The End Result of Adolescence

In adolescence the outcome, regarding stability and ultimate integration, depends upon (*a*) the way in which the depressive position has been worked through in infancy, (*b*) the qualitative and quantitative importance and internal topographical situation of the main fixations (in particular it is important whether freedom is allowed or whether the fixations are rigid, and in what fields of activity, intrapsychic or interpersonal), and (*c*) destructive factors in quantitative and qualitative and also topographical or situational aspects (for example the strength of aggression and hatred versus love; life instinct versus death instinct: or the strength of primal envy which is related to the death instinct).

At all times of crisis during life, beginning with the early crisis of the depressive position where the mother is recognised for the first time as a person rather than a composite of parts, there is an opportunity of working over the depressive position again. Such an opportunity occurs during adolescence.

One of the difficulties with, and for, the adolescent is the pattern of change both on a very short-term basis, that is from mood to mood, and also with a very much longer rhythm, that of development. The rapidly switching situation confronts the adolescent himself with a constant challenge to his various adaptive mechanisms. He easily becomes a displaced person. The authorities, including perhaps particularly the parents, who have to deal with the adolescent, never quite know with whom they are dealing at any given moment. Sometimes it is the philosopher, sometimes the clamouring baby, and sometimes the young delinquent. The more slow rhythm of change is of course from early to middle to late adolescence and then on into adult life. Human development does not take place in a steady smooth way but usually by a series of fits and starts, some of which involve the whole of the personality of the individual, and some of which involve only part of it. An adolescent, for example, may develop the wish for and the capacity to use freedom in one sphere of life and to lack it in another; in

37

other words the rebel, young adult, and the clamouring baby may be present all at the same time and all competing for the attention and control of the headquarter-self of the adolescent. I think it is this instability and insecurity of the headquarter-self which makes crystallisation of personal identity so important, so often a need which ends up in one or more crises before ultimate resolution, and something which taxes the skill of the various networks dealing with adolescent problems to the utmost.

One of the greatest disservices which can be done to adolescents is to give them a legitimate grievance. Being wronged helps them to abdicate from ownership of responsibility into a feeling of being wronged and being persecuted. In other words there is a sliding down the scale from a state dominated by depressive anxiety to one which is pervaded by persecutory anxiety. It is in this aggrieved state that a lot of adolescent delinquency takes place. Also it is this stage, often expressed in the form of a complete lack of confidence and faith in adults, particularly the parents, teachers and adult leaders, which leads an adolescent or rather facilitates his turning to the false gods of drugs, drink and delinquency. All three false lines of pseudo-development are intensified if there is a peer group in which these activities are regarded as part of the norm. In this case there is generally further regression, an accentuation of antidevelopmental trends, and a reduction of guilt by sharing it with the rest of the peer group. Also in the presence of a peer group which provides something akin to a subculture, the communication with parents, teachers and other responsible persons tends to be reduced to a minimum and even that is often on a formal rather than a realistic basis. Not all peer groups, of course, are destructive. Sometimes the adolescent is confronted with parents and other authority figures who, despite protests to the contrary, are really punitive, restrictive, envious and in general antidevelopmental. The turning to a peer group may then be essential if the adolescent is to go on with any kind of satisfactory development.

Using the caring and therapeutic services in the first place as extensions of the family and social interactive network can be effective in a number of cases, probably a very large number. In this way the situation is as it was in battle conditions when the adaptive capacities of a number of relatively healthy men were overwhelmed, but if applied soon enough the restoration of those adaptive capacities to reasonably effective functioning was not difficult to achieve.

Normal Adolescence?

It will be seen that there is no hard and fast line between the normal and the pathological, but if there is too much previously laid down pathology, the likelihood of breakdown during adolescence is great. The problem could hinge on whether the earlier difficulties have been worked through to resolution. In this case the individual is likely to be strengthened. When the earlier difficulties have been incompletely worked through and therefore have had to be repressed or split off, the individual has a problem which may be reactivated under certain conditions, and complicate or at least add to difficulties when they arise in adolescence.

The most difficult part of writing a chapter on adolescence is to separate what is part of the normal process of change and development from the pathology of adolescence. When turbulence and distress settle down again after some use of family and social interactive networks, one cannot regard the disturbance, however florid, as an illness in the sense of a definite nosological entity. There is one other way of assessing whether or not a disturbed phase is part of an illness or a storm in the course of normal development, and that is by its effect on growth and maturation. If growth and maturation proceed as well or perhaps better when turbulence subsides, one has probably been dealing with something which cannot be considered to be part of an illness. The idea which now crystallises is that what constitutes pathology or illness is a state in which the adaptive capabilities of the adolescent are overwhelmed and will not right themselves again with the simple removal of the stress.

It will be seen, therefore, that too soft a life is one which has not stimulated and challenged the individual in the use and development of his adaptive mechanisms, and too hard a life is one in which stresses have been so massive or so manifold, falling so thick and fast upon the individual, that his adaptive capacity is completely overwhelmed.

It may sound like a contradiction of terms, but many crises are *normal* in adolescence, and in fact necessary. It depends on the degree and whether the crises help or hinder development of necessary areas of the personality. Without doldrums, pain, hurt, experiment, stimulation, aggression, tenderness, flatness, excitement, defiance, exaltation, responsibility, concern, love, hate, mood swings, rebellion etc., it would not be adolescence. That is, adolescence without normative crises is not adolescence.

Out of struggle, trial and error, out of risks and opportunities, comes adulthood. Out of the crises of healthy change comes, eventually, maturity.

3

Adolescence and Change

MARY CAPES

Much has been written already in this book about the changes which occur as part of a natural and normal process of development during adolescence, and of how these may become modified or exaggerated. In this chapter an attempt is made to pick out certain more general features of adolescence, look at its overall pattern and achieve some kind of perspective about the subject, which is often so highly charged.

It has to be remembered, however, in regard to the following sections that the division of body from mind, of intelligence from emotion, of heredity from environmental influences is inevitably an artificial one. In the end it is the individual, the sum total of these many aspects, whom we must consider.

Physical Changes

This period between childhood and maturity is accompanied by more changes than at any other time of life, with the exception of the infant years, the other equally short but supremely important period of development. Unlike the early years, though, the physical, intellectual and emotional changes are more erratic, there is need for greater conscious adaptation, and, for the first time, certain phases of growth will have reached their limit. The adolescent who is uneasy about his size or his physique or about his level of intellectual functioning has to face the fact that by the age of twenty relatively few further changes are likely to occur. And, prior to this, he may already have had to make adjustments to a sudden increase in height of four or five inches even before puberty, or, at the opposite end of the scale, to remaining undersized until a spurt of growth around the age of eighteen. Confusing matters further, the onset of puberty, associated by most people with the start of menstruation in girls and the first seminal emissions in boys, may not necessarily develop in parallel with any physical growth in either sex. Girls, for example, whose menstruation has not commenced until after seventeen or eighteen, may be taller than those who start much sooner. How much easier it would be for the adolescent if these changes were predictable and followed a more even course. The agonies some young people endure about their breast development or the size of their penis in early adolescence when they have to undress for games or other sport amongst a crowd of schoolmates deserves much greater understanding than it often gets. Adults should help not only by making these anomalies more clearly understood but by adopting a philosophic attitude whenever extremes bedevil their children. And many a slow developer passes through a phase of attention-seeking and apparent aggressiveness in the year or two before the final spurt of growth, only for these problems to resolve themselves when normal height is reached.

The Intelligence

Whilst physical growth is proceeding on its even or less even course, profound changes are also taking place in the development of the intelligence. Mental growth is now recognised as continuing until the age of twenty, after that a gradual and slow decline becomes evident in certain tests which require speed and flexibility, but those involving general information or certain special skills obviously depend on continuing maturity. One of the problems in measuring intelligence, of course, is that the ability to use words is at a premium in most tests while other special abilities such as creativeness and the 'imaginative searching after truth' cannot so far be adequately assessed (if they ever will be). The fact that mental growth does not reach its peak of development until twenty shows that any early decisions about educational streaming at fourteen or fifteen are regrettable. Skills at science and mathematics, for example, may only emerge at fifteen or sixteen and only then provided the opportunities are made available for them to flourish. Continuing development also makes sense of the later school-leaving age if the extra years are used to spark off and foster broader interests, interests in the process of living, the nature of human relationships, the use of leisure, as well as more strictly academic subjects. For one of the great changes in intellectual development is in the growing capacity to think in abstract terms and become receptive of opinions different from one's own. Heaven knows, this is difficult enough, even when the emotions are least involved, but not usually until fourteen or fifteen are the processes of thinking in abstracts fully developed. From this age onwards, discussion and debate, testing out the provocative, the ability to listen and to understand that others may legitimately have a different viewpoint are the hallmarks of a growing maturity. By the same token, intelligent and thoughtful parents, in their effort to instil into their young children values and beliefs, tend at times to talk in terms which are far beyond their comprehension at an earlier age.

Piaget[1] has described these decisive changes in the following terms:

'Around the age of seven or eight, the child discovers what we shall call concrete operations (classification, serialisation, spatial operations and the like) ... the great novelty that characterises adolescent thought and that starts around the age of eleven to twelve, but does not reach its point of equilibrium until the age of fourteen or fifteen ... consists in detaching the concrete logic from the objects themselves, so that it can function on verbal or symbolic

43

statements without other support. ... In a word, the adolescent is an individual who is capable (and this is where he reaches the level of the adult) of building or understanding ideal or abstract theories and concepts ... these intellectual transformations typical of the adolescent's thinking enable him not only to achieve his integration into the social relationship of adults ... but also to conquer a certain number of fundamental intellectual operations which constitute the basis for a scientific education at high school level.'

All this is assuming that the youngster has been growing up in an environment where conversation, books and the purposes of education are valued; where these interests are minimal as in under-privileged homes, thinking remains at a concrete rather than an abstract level into adulthood and will remain so unless the additional stimulus is provided.

Emotional Changes

Even when physical and intellectual growth proceeds smoothly and without undue stress, there still remains the major task of achieving some degree of emotional maturity by the age of eighteen or nineteen. This, in effect, means that the earlier dependency on the family has to be outgrown, dependency on the peer group (with its temporary dominance) has also to be lived through largely by trial and error to a stage of reaching some sense of personal identity. Maturity in the end shows itself in the refusal to exploit another individual, and, in a heterosexual relationship, in the fusion of tenderness with desire. To attain such a maturity during only six or seven years of adolescence requires a monumental change of attitude, and a profound 'internal rearrangement' of emotions which at best is likely to lead to swings of mood and to erratic behaviour. And from time immemorial adolescence has been regarded as a stormy period, characterised by rejection of parental authority, contempt for the established order and 'disrespect for elders'. Shakespeare as usual hits the nail on the head when he makes the old shepherd say, 'I would there were no age between ten and twenty-three, or that youth would sleep out the rest; for there is nothing in the between but getting wenches with child, wronging the ancientry, stealing, fighting' (*Winter's Tale*, Act III, Scene iii). That was nearly 400 years ago but this image of adolescence has remained unchanged throughout the ages, and to judge by the headlines in the news media, continues today much as in the past. A new note, however, has crept in recently with the advent of the computer and other devices for collecting information from a vast body of people. Douvan and Adelson[2] in their study of over 3,000 American young people found somewhat surprisingly little of the turmoil, the conflict and instability normally attributed to this group. On the contrary, they were rather staid, unimaginative and conservative in their attitudes and ready to avoid rather than foster conflicts and arguments. These investigators expressed some concern at the absence of 'the passions, the restlessness, the vivacity' which they regarded as a healthy requisite to normal maturation rather than any concern about evidence of asocial behaviour. And Offer[3] in an intensive study of a smaller number, who were particularly chosen for their normality, also found a surprising degree of conservatism, an almost total absence of turmoil and a sturdy response in the face of any family stress.

Meissner,[4] who approached the subject from a somewhat different angle, asked over a thousand thirteen to eighteen year-old high school boys to describe their attitude to their parents and to their home life. He too found the great majority, far from demonstrating any generation gap, were proud of their parents, enjoyed inviting their friends to meet them and were happy to be at home. Eighty-four per cent spent half or more of their leisure-time at home until nearing the end of adolescene, and not until this age did they seriously want to get away from home and resist parental control. The disengagement had been a gradual one, with little evidence of rebelliousness or conflict.

Turning more specifically to sexual behaviour, Schofield[5] (1965) in a study of nearly 2,000 fifteen to nineteen-year-old boys and girls from varied backgrounds in London found

45

that not more than a fifth of the boys and a tenth of the girls in the age group had experienced sexual intercourse. This figure may have increased somewhat in past years but there is still no evidence to suggest that promiscuity or casual sexual experiences are generally condoned by young people.

Investigations such as these tend to confirm Horrocks's[6] opinion that

> if the environment is such that the adolescent can gradually be inducted into experiences for which he is prepared and with which he is able to cope, if he is allowed to assume responsibility and play a mature role when he is ready to do so, and if there is a real effort on the part of adults to accept his interests and, where possible, to meet his needs, the adolescent will find his transition into maturity comparatively smooth and uncomplicated'.

Professor Weiner gives a masterly survey of the many studies of normality and abnormality in his book *Psychological Disturbance in Adolescence*[7] and draws similar conclusions to those of Horrocks.

External Changes

Reassurance based on such factual information about adolescence must help parents to avoid undue anxiety in spite of the barrage from the news media and the long-standing and traditional fears and expectations. There is a risk, however, in an effort to paint the picture in perspective and bring out the more positive aspects, that it will be too static and fail to depict the changing scene. So rapid are the changes that only the most tenuous outlines can convey anything approximately near the truth.

The contrast between the biological changes which unfold themselves in an almost universal pattern and the cultural influences which are far from universal, and which change so quickly and dramatically, is the main thesis of this chapter. During only the last few years, for example, travel has become possible to almost anywhere one chooses; news which once took months to reach its destination is seen or heard in millions of homes within a matter of minutes, and information can be gathered on an unprecedented scale.

It has become possible not only to study a variety of patterns of child-rearing and note the end-results in both primitive and highly complex societies, but also to collect the views of an unlimited number of individuals of any age group and of any shade of opinion, and disseminate these findings the world over. The customs of the grandparents in all their variation, traditionally handed down to parents and by them to their sons and daughters, no longer hold as they used to, except in the most isolated communities. Change and technical developments are so rapid that not infrequently it is the young (at least in the less industrialised places) who have to instruct their parents instead of the other way round, and so their roles become reversed.

No one has described all this more vividly than the anthropologist, Margaret Mead,[8] in her book *Culture and Commitment*, when she discusses the so-called generation gap and the main cultural influences to which the teenager is now exposed. The culture which she calls the post-figurative one, characteristic of human societies for millenia, in which children learnt primarily from their forebears by word of mouth and by example, and unquestioningly and unconsciously absorbed the expectations of the old, is now disappearing.

With the development of complex civilisations, either with the subjugation of other societies, or with rapid technological advances outstripping the knowledge of the older members, or when migration enforces new patterns of behaviour, new cultural patterns must inevitably evolve. The model for this kind of society rests in the behaviour of contemporaries rather than the elders; this cofigurative culture, at its simplest, is one where no grandparents are present, and the past has become shadowy and distorted. For continuity in all cultures must depend on the living presence of three generations, and on the general assumption that the way of life will remain eternally the same.

When cofiguration among those of similar age becomes institutionalised, one finds the phenomenon of a teenage culture, and she describes this situation for the present-day American teenager thus:

'The culture-wide effects of cofiguration began to be felt by the beginning of the twentieth century. The nuclear family was established, a close relationship to the grandparents was no longer expected of grandchildren, and parents, as they lost their position of dominance, handed over to children the task of setting their own standards. By 1920, style setting was beginning to pass to the mass media, in the name of each successive adolescent group, and parental discipline was passing to an increasingly unsympathetic and embattled community. . . . Culturally, cofiguration had become the dominant, prevailing mode. Few of the elderly pretended to have any relationship to the contemporary culture. Parents, however grudgingly, expected to accede to the urgent demands their children were taught to make, not by the school or by other, more acculturated children, but by the mass media.'

This perhaps is an extreme picture of teenage culture. Others may still regard this as a subculture, holding that a strong element of post-figurative characteristics survive at a deeper level for expression later when maturity is reached. However, with worldwide intercommunication, easy travel and constant technological change, the young everywhere can, and frequently do, share something which their elders have never known, and the older generation on their part have lived through and experienced changes which will never be repeated. Such a situation between the generations is entirely new, and knows no boundaries.

Margaret Mead foresees the evolution of a third culture which she describes as a prefigurative one. She urges the older generations to alter their attitudes and no longer set out to teach their children what to learn since they no longer know the answers, but instead to teach them how to learn— 'not what they should be committed to, but the value of commitment', moving in this way towards the creation of open systems that focus on the future and on the child as yet unborn. The essential in such an emerging culture is to build an environment in which a child can feel secure and yet be free to discover himself and the world at large.

Change in Adolescent Attitudes

Not so long ago, in the 1950s, adolescents were constantly being criticised for their superficiality, for their exclusive concern with athletic skill or social success with their peers, or for the vast sums of money they spent on trivia. Today, some twenty years later, they are criticised for their 'permissive' behaviour, particularly in the sexual sphere, their casual attitude to work, and their carefree style of dress.

They are the first generation who on a massive scale have been able to use the telephone, the motorbike and the car to rendezvous where they will, with whom they will of their own age-group, and spend hours enjoying pop music. Yet recent surveys have also shown a much greater seriousness about learning; on average the student population has doubled in all the major countries of the world since 1950 and these adolescents increasingly want to know more about themselves as individuals, about what makes them tick, and about their relationships with others. An increasingly honest and direct approach leads them to question the value of bureaucratic orderliness and the status quo, and with this less rigid and conventional attitude comes a greater compassion and understanding of the underprivileged seldom known before in industrialised communities. The growing emphasis on achieving academic skill and getting diplomas and degrees does, however, lead to a considerable split between those who take up jobs immediately on leaving school and receive an increasingly sizeable weekly wage, and those who live on relatively limited grants for anything up to ten years after embarking on their careers.

But, lest this all sounds too earnest, we must not forget the thousands of young people who come together in public park and private field 'to salute the midsummer sun in its rising and its setting'[9] at their pop festivals. These events, available to all classes and nationalities, are astonishingly happy and

49

good-natured occasions when only a very small minority behave in a discordant or antisocial manner.

Maybe in years to come, if anyone should bother to read this chapter, he may think the emphasis on change and its attendant difficulties has been considerably exaggerated; he will at least agree that man's relationship with man was forever altered in the mid-twentieth century, associated with the less than enthusiastic attitude of the young as a whole to technocracy, to material success and to exploitation. Present-day adolescents, when they consider their parents' world, see it as dominated by vast business enterprises, by power blocks, by scientific expertise and by ever more complex machinery. They see man as ceasing to work hand in hand with nature but rather, in arrogance, ignoring it. They see their parents, in the main, as tense and unrelaxed, anxious to better the lives of their children but under a system which is intolerant of any individuality. Their teenagers then pin on buttons declaring 'I am a human being—do not mutilate, spindle or tear' or 'Make love not war'!

But, as in the past, it is the minority, though not only the most incorrigible and dissident youngsters, who largely hit the headlines and get the attention of the mass media. Amongst these are the groups who express their resentment that, under pressure of numbers in the universities, the tutor-pupil relationship no longer holds good, or who show their disapproval of the prevailing family patterns or the more conventional and sterile means of earning a livelihood, and choose to live in communes. Others in the Western world, disenchanted with their parents' religious practices, seek out the more mystical experiences of the East. At its most extreme, others escape into complete anonymity by running away (and one can run very great distances these days) and ultimately destroy themselves with drugs. Most worrying are those who, feeling they have nothing to lose, resort to wanton destruction and violence as a means of drawing attention to their cause, or as an expression of their total alienation.

Some of these protesters have known no security or affection in their most impressionable early years, others have grown up in stifling and deadening environments, others have been too gently nurtured and are ill-prepared for the realities of a more demanding world, and many in one way or another are grossly disturbed. The question often arises as to whether there is more disturbance and mental illness in adolescents now than in the past. Certainly the number seeking help has increased in leaps and bounds, but so has the number of adolescents making up the total population, and, to a lesser extent, more facilities for treatment have also become available. There is as yet no answer. What has been shown by Lee Robins,[10] Masterson[11] and the writer of this chapter, to mention but a few, is that the history of disturbance seldom arises *de novo* during adolescence but is mostly a long one extending back to the earliest years of childhood. An unsatisfactory emotional climate, whether of restlessness and insecurity, cold indifference on the part of the parents or excessive indulgence during the highly vulnerable first few years, crops up time and time again in the histories of the disturbed youngsters, particularly in those who are violently aggressive and who 'act-out' in an antisocial and destructive manner.

In the United States, for example, where the figures are known, over 50 per cent of the population is now under twenty-five years of age and any increase in disaffiliation through lack of attention to the early years and through lack of parental rapport might in due course lead to an alarming proportion of anarchic behaviour.

This lack of *rapport* was demonstrated by the Harvard Laboratory of Human Development[12] in a comparatively recent survey of American and Danish adolescents when they were asked to whom they would go for advice when in difficulties, whether to teachers, parents, or counsellors. Neither in Denmark nor America did more than 40 per cent choose to consult an adult, and that was more for advice about practical issues such as schooling, career decisions and clothes. Less than 40 per cent wished to discuss their personal problems or any moral issues with an adult. A similar enquiry in Czechoslovakia revealed even fewer adults featuring in this way.

We, the older generation, are often baffled, frequently become angry and impatient, sometimes are appalled by the minority groups. We may respond by becoming more authoritarian, we may opt out completely, or we may attempt to share our children's lives by trying to become more adolescent than they themselves—often living vicariously through them. We are too uncertain to assert the old standards, and have little to offer in their place. We know we cannot put the clock back even if we want to, and, if we are honest with ourselves, we must admit that much that has happened in the last fifty years is as appalling as at any time in history; it seems the young on the whole are making a brave attempt to go one better. It is not necessary to read a 'way-out' journal to be reminded of this; we have only to turn to that journal of the Establishment, *The Times* :

'Our dry, impersonal, metropolitan, mechanised, commercial society, with too little love and too limited a passion, is not a satisfactory envelope for human being. The real merit of our civilisation is dribbling away through our fingers. As with the early nineteenth-century Romantics, whom they so closely resemble, some of the leaders of the young will destroy themselves with drugs or disordered sexuality or other forms of despair. But the rejection by the stronger spirits who survive of what is most degrading in our society will influence their generation and our future.

'The young of 1971 will push Britain towards objectives which are aesthetic, idealist and humane, at the expense of other objectives which are materialist, powerful and profitable. How far they will succeed in changing the balance, and how quickly, is much more difficult to know.'[13]

It is essential for us of the older generation to recognise that we are now living in an ambience which is entirely new and hardly explored as yet, it is equally essential for us to overcome our inevitable sense of loneliness and disarray and meet with the young as one individual with another, to debate with them about values and about hopes and discuss with them how to get on with the potentially exciting process of living in a very stimulating and still lovely world.

REFERENCES

1. J. Piaget, 'Intellectual Development of the Adolescent', *Adolescence: Psychosocial Perspectives*, G. Caplan and S. Lebovici (eds) (New York and London, Basic Books Inc., 1969), p. 22.
2. E. Douvan and J. Adelson, *The Adolescent Experience* (New York, Wiley, 1966), pp. 351–4.
3. D. Offer, *The Psychological World of the Teenager* (New York and London, Basic Books Inc., 1969).
4. W. W. Meissner, 'Parental Interreaction of the Adolescent Boy', *Journal of Genetic Psychology*, Vol. 107 (1965), pp. 225–33.
5. M. Schofield, *The Sexual Behaviour of Young People* (London, Longmans Green; and Boston, Little, Brown, 1965).
6. J. E. Horrocks, 'The Adolescent', *Manual of Child Psychology*, L. Carmichael (ed.) (New York, Wiley, 2nd edn, 1954), pp. 697–734.
7. I. B. Weiner, *Psychological Disturbance in Adolescence* (London, Sydney, Toronto and New York, John Wiley & Sons, 1970).
8. Margaret Mead, *Culture and Commitment*, *A Study of the Generation Gap* (London, Bodley Head Ltd., 1970, Panther Books, 1972).
9. T. Roszak, *The Making of a Counter-Culture*, *Reflections on the Technocratic Society and Its Youthful Opposition* (London, Faber & Faber, 1970), p. 149.
10. L. N. Robins, *Deviant Children Grow Up* (Baltimore, Williams & Wilkins, 1966).
11. J. F. Masterson, Jun., *The Psychiatric Dilemma of Adolescence* (London, J. & A. Churchill, 1967).
12. Derek Miller, 'Parental Responsibility for Adolescent Maturity', *The Family and its Future*, K. Elliott (ed.) (London, CIBA Foundation Symposium, J. & A. Churchill, 1970) p. 37.
13. *The Times* (28 April, 1971).

4

Adolescence and the Family

JOHN BYNG-HALL and MARILYN J. MILLER

Introduction

The shock of adolescent change produces vibrations which resonate with the 'adolescence' inside parents, muffled perhaps by the intervening years, but nevertheless pulsating. The tune or cacophony produced does not stop at the front door but strikes chords in the community at large. Society's response impinges back on each family, increasing either harmony or dissonance as the case may be. With this cycle in mind we are going to start by exploring some ideas about the interplay between inner world and family patterns and attempt to illustrate these by describing a family scene and its dynamics. Finally, we will go on to examine how the family and society may influence each other.

Family Dramas: Scenes and Inner Scripts

Much of each member's inner fantasy is taken up with an endless variety of dramas and plots involving family inter-actions. This inner life draws on memories and perceptions; some accurate, some edited, some distorted. Thus it is constantly being added to from ·the everyday experience of family life. Inner imagination then elaborates or completes a scene to give it some meaning and a possible role for the self to enact in the drama. Tragedy as well as supreme delight can be the outcome of some of these inner dramas. Particularly from the child's distorted and diminutive viewpoint, the imaginings can be terrifying; although parents can also be terrified by their images of adolescents. Many of the more primitive, calamitous, painful or forbidden phantasies are kept out of awareness for much of the time. The particular script colours the view each person has of what is happening, etched in by fantasy.* How much do either 'nightmare' or idealised aspects of inner life determine action? Can primitive distorted images be modified by experience? These are both crucial questions.

From one viewpoint, the family provides a setting in which inner erroneous assumptions can be corrected. From the other, shared family misperceptions and illusions can reinforce each other over the years, eventually becoming enshrined as 'truths'. Some focus will be made on this latter aspect, firstly because these distorted family beliefs may cause problems, and, secondly, because adolescents have a disconcerting tendency to challenge accepted assumptions, throwing the family into flux.

Mutual Defence: Achilles Plus his Heel

As clinicians, we focus on features which lead to pain, distress or failure to grow. Family interactions can become repetitive and stereotyped. We need to ask ourselves why, because this can lead to an inability to adapt to new situations, such as, the blossoming sexuality of adolescents. Individuals can become caught in rigid strait-jackets when they repress or deny intolerably painful or forbidden feelings. One very common piece of self-deception is to disown the 'bad' aspects as belonging to 'him not me'. People can then band together on the basis of 'it is them not us'. Alternatively, the group or couple may find a scapegoat within its own ranks.

* In this chapter, unless otherwise stated, the term *f*antasy will mean conscious and unconscious fantasy, whereas *ph*antasy will always be unconscious.

Falling in love is an exciting, idealising process, but some writers, such as Dicks,[1] suggest that selecting a permanent partner may also involve finding a person who can represent the repudiated part of the self. This provides an opportunity, after the intense idealising has worn off, of refinding oneself in the other, or, alternatively, for attacking the 'bad' part in the partner, thus using the spouse as a scapegoat. The brash way in which adolescents challenge established value systems also makes them ready targets for family scapegoating. To summarise, repudiation often involves three stages; firstly, pushing experiences out of self-awareness, then attributing them to someone else, and finally creating a social matrix which will continue to support this displacement. The whole family then develops a particular stereotyped pattern for avoiding themes which touch on a specific raw area. New ways of dealing with this area are resisted by all, if each person is using the system to defend himself against pain.

Although mutual defence may push much of the repudiated theme out of awareness, what may be unconscious phantasy in one member may be conscious fantasy for another. Elements of the theme may have been openly manifest in the history of the family, say, a desertion or mental breakdown, a violent episode, etc., and indeed the topic can probably be spotted somewhere in the present behaviour or imagery used by family members. Thus a theme is often woven deeply into the whole fabric of the family, past and present; body and soul; each member facing it—albeit in his own particular way.

Family mutual defences are often created by setting up a family organisation which emphasises the opposite—or at least sharply in contrast to—the repudiated theme. For instance, to help avoid a theme of desertion—the family may build up a tradition of close togetherness' with strong rules against leaving, thus creating a self image or *family myth* of 'we never leave each other', but like many myths it may contain only part of the truth, obscuring a contrasting facet. Many of these 'we will stick together for ever' families nurse secret wishes to leave. Threats of desertion are quite commonly used—after all it is the most feared punishment—and actual desertion may have occurred.

Myths have two main dimensions, one referring to the present, 'it *is* a myth that . . .', the second refers to the past; the legends that the family tells and retells about itself. These particular family stories are chosen, and probably moulded, in order to explain how the repudiated themes appeared, why they needed to be controlled, and the way in which this was done. In this way the legends of the past support the stance of today. For example, stories about the 'wicked deserter' and how the remaining family bravely closed ranks carries important messages for the present. If the continuing inclination to leave each other is revealed, the myth might be expected to shatter, but this does not give enough credit to the power and effectiveness of the myth. The rules set up by it become entrenched within individuals' superegos, which drag each back into the family through guilt.

Ferreira[2] was the first to describe family myths and pointed out that all families probably need them. They provide useful blueprints for action, but those families which are overburdened with mythology run into difficulties because of the rigidity imposed. Byng-Hall[3] explored some of the origins of the family myths and how they were related, in particular, to the parents' need to defend themselves. Offspring have changing requirements. Children need the family unit and a myth such as 'we never leave each other' as their ally. Adolescents need to leave so they must shatter that particular myth. For long Achilles was powerful and miraculously defended; the arrow eventually found his vulnerable heel. One point at which repudiated themes may emerge is in a family row or scene. Adolescents may be searching for and finding chinks in the armour.

A Typical Family Scene

The Hardy's are usually a co-operative family and show warmth and concern for each other. Occasionally, however, things boil up. It is Sunday lunchtime and Mrs Hardy has just taken a tray up to her mother, Mrs Green, who is ill in bed. The rest of the family have started eating, except for Jane, aged fourteen, who arrives late, and scrapes her chair noisily as she sits down. She makes no apology for her lateness, or for the fact that she is still in her dressing-gown. She gets an angry glare from her mother, but no one else seems to notice her arrival.

Mrs Hardy, a plump and powerful-looking woman, has a harassed and weary air. She bangs a plate of food down in front of Jane, who starts eating apparently ignoring her mother's aggression. After a few mouthfuls, Jane begins to toy with her food irritatingly. Peter, the thirteen-year-old son, looks uneasy, glances at his father, and starts talking about a project he is doing at school. Father, who had been studiously looking at his nearly empty plate, responds with some relief. The two males have a rather hollow discussion. Only the four-year-old Mandy seems at ease, taking in the whole scene as she greedily gobbles down the last mouthfuls of her pudding. She starts to kick Jane under the table. Father tells her to stop. Jane pretends to ignore her and Mandy switches to another tack. 'I had the biggest pudding. . . . Mummy said I could . . . she gave me yours 'cos you were late.' This time, Jane lashes out with an angry kick at Mandy, and gets up to leave the table. Mother says 'sit down and eat your meal'. Jane flounces away to the record-player and says, 'I didn't want any anyway.' Mother gives Mr Hardy a look clearly demanding action. He looks extremely uncomfortable but avoids her gaze. Jane does not obey her mother but puts a record on. Mr Hardy looks at his wife and says defeatedly, 'Oh, leave her alone . . . it's Sunday. Can't we have some peace?'

Mrs Hardy responds angrily with the retort that it might be peace for him, but not for her. She has cooked the dinner. She will leave for ever if she's not appreciated. There is a tense hush. Peter and his father exchange glances. Mandy's drumming feet stop still. Jane unseen by mother glances heavenward as if to say 'here we go again'. Mrs Hardy, surveying the scene, is only partially satisfied with the impact of her threat, and switches to a new tack. She was worrying half the night about Jane and what had made her so late. 'It's not safe for a girl of fourteen to be out till three in the morning. Whatever could she be doing?' Mr Hardy offers an unconvincing comment, 'She can look after herself.' This far from stems the tide, his wife goes on to the ill-effects of all this noise and worry on grandmother. 'It will be the death of her. . . . Put that thing off,' she shrieks at Jane. Jane retorts that her mother's shrieking is making more noise than the record-player and retreats into a sulky but triumphant posture.

Mrs Hardy clears the table noisily, ignoring Peter's seemingly innocent protest that he has not finished. Mandy, quiet now, slides on to father's lap, starts sucking her thumb and watches the whole scene with anxious fascination. The music blares and Peter talks to his father who, by now, can scarcely pretend to listen. Peter however seems to want to ignore what is going on around him, and to bury himself in a tale of the latest chemistry experiment at school. In a serious tone, he issues forth long names of chemical substances, foreign to his father. As he does so, he adds colour to make it more exciting, and hopefully to capture the weary attention of his one remaining parent. He describes 'a bubbling' and a 'smoking dangerous mixture', and finally an explosion. Father, hardly listening, replies mechanically 'that sounds very interesting'. Peter, now in a world of fantasy, promotes father's anxiety further, in a desperate attempt to get his share of attention: 'One chap lost an eye a few years back.' There is silence as father ponders on the doubtful truth of that statement. His face indicates that he is not fooled. He turns sharply back to Jane, and loudly orders her to go and help her mother with the washing-up. Mother also calls to Jane who finally flounces out to help, leaving the record-player blaring in the other room lest attention be turned away in her absence.

Dynamics of Family Scenes

These family encounters can provide important pivotal points in a family's history. Adolescents are particularly likely to provoke scenes and rows. In this way they discover what parents are really like. They uncover fears, anxieties and prejudices and they challenge myths. The family may negotiate new, fresher life-styles in a row, but sometimes there is a backlash. From our point of view, family rows are interesting because repudiated themes may surface, old myths may crumble and new myths crystalise.

Meal times can reach flashpoint in some families. In giving, taking, or refusing food, we reach back to our most fundamental early primitive selves, stirring the most intense feelings. Feeding can become a language of emotion: a battle-ground for conflict, past and present, as well as an exquisite, loving art.

Mrs Hardy had been starved as a child, not so much of food as of attention. She had to share her tired parents' love with seven siblings. Food became the symbol for gratification of her longing. The intense yearning for love could turn into bitter rage if not fulfilled, but when she had been angry her mother had banished her from the room or threatened to desert her. She had to bury her rage very deep. Through her own marriage and children she had striven to heal the wound, with a fair measure of success. Mother's caring as well as her proverbial 'puddings' had become woven into the family mythology.

Jane therefore struck mother a cruel blow merely by being late for meals. In the Hardy children's battle for attention, Mandy knew she could provoke her mother's anger against Jane. Not satisfied with mother merely banging the plate down in front of Jane, Mandy needled Jane with kicks but eventually unnervingly found her mark with the topic of food. She could rely on igniting Jane's jealousy by eating Jane's share of Mum's pud. This would equally predictably spark off a battle between Jane and her mother. It was, of course, only half a victory for Mandy. Parental attention as well as anger went to Jane, who was becoming an expert at achieving the double: expressing her independence plus keeping parental concern by refusing food.

Jane introduced the additional topic of sex by coming down in her dressing-gown following a very late night. Adolescents can set up a resonance with unfulfilled wishes

60

buried by their parents at the time of their own youth. Mrs
Hardy had become a second mother to her younger brothers
during her adolescence, but had escaped the home in her late
teens by marrying her first boyfriend. Thus she had never
experienced a gay and free time. When Jane started dating it
stirred mother's forbidden longings. Mrs Hardy was able to
relive some rebellious sexuality vicariously through Jane.
She constantly probed Jane for details of her sex life,
ostensibly in order to put a stop to whatever was going on.
Jane knew exactly how to provoke her mother's curiosity:
coming in late and withholding information did the trick
magnificently. Needless to say, this stimulated her father's
feelings as well. He had been too timid to have more than the
one girlfriend whom he then married. Imagining the lustful
behaviour of Jane's numerous boyfriends, and then furiously
condemning them for these imagined activities, enabled him
to re-experience hidden longings but simultaneously to
disown them. One of the sources of his timidity with girls
was the force with which he had had to repudiate any sexual
feelings whatever for his mother. To re-experience any
incestuous impulses was for him particularly taboo.

Anger also reverberated round the room. Some could
openly express it like mother and Jane. Mandy was content
to provoke it. It was the two males who found it most difficult. Immediately they saw a storm brewing they attempted,
led by Peter, to divert the conversation on to school topics. In
practice both were timid quiet people. Peter, as he showed
through his imagery of explosions, was highly preoccupied
with the topic of violence, as are many boys of his age. How
is he to express his rising tide of anger? Who will control it?
Will it devastate and destroy if let loose? These anxieties
resonated disturbingly with father's own rebellious anger,
which had been ruled out of court in his teens because his
own father could not tolerate naked aggression. Mr Hardy's
anxiety, demonstrated by his avoidance of confrontations,
confirmed Peter's own fears. The male's inner preoccupation
with violence resonated with increasing amplitude with the
family fury over deprivation. Peter and his father both felt
safer if the women expressed the anger. Mr Hardy could

61

have calmed his wife's fury by responding to her repeated pleas to control Jane. Instead she was allowed to become increasingly irascible until she was faced with her own deep fears about anger. Initially she dipped back into her past for the effective controlling weapon: a threat of desertion. Although partially successful, it did not rally her family to her side. This then faced her with her innermost, unconscious, dread that her anger might kill her mother. This fear had been rubbed in in childhood by her mother, Mrs Green, with statements like, 'You'll be the death of me.' In the present, Mrs Green was ill and had been very demanding. Part of Mrs Hardy secretly wished that she would die. Jane became a very convenient scapegoat for this wish. Mother felt that it was Jane's difficult behaviour and noise, not her own impulses, which would kill grandmother. Jane saw through this as quick as a flash triumphantly pointing out that mother's shriek was even noisier! Needless to say, mother chose to miss that point.

Adolescents frequently challenge parental defences but paradoxically also support them by behaving as suitable scapegoats. Jane had clearly done this with her mother's anger and sexuality.

Outcome of Family Rows

Many of the Hardy's anxiety-ridden themes were now in the open. It is at this point in a family history that there is potential for shift which may be towards either growth or further petrification. More needs to be known about the factors which determine the direction taken, because the fulcrum of mental health lies in this area.

The Hardy family was balanced at a point where mother might have attacked father, completely undermining his shaky self-esteem. However, she held her tongue because there was considerable anxiety about father collapsing into a jelly-like state. This fear stemmed from the fact that both parents had fathers who were vulnerable under pressure. Thus both spouses feared this and were determined to support an image of a reliable competent father in their present family. Mr Hardy fitted the role required by being a bank clerk.

In the family scene parental authority was flaunted by Jane. At first Mr Hardy sensed that Jane would disobey him, and hence he avoided a potentially unsuccessful confrontation. As we have seen, he also delayed his intervention because he was getting something out of his wife's rising fury. Mrs Hardy's outburst, followed by her departure from the room, relieved the tension somewhat. At this point Peter enabled his father to re-establish authority by escalating his own explosive imagery to unlikely levels at which point Mr Hardy took note and then firmly relegated Peter's ideas to the realms of fantasy. This relieved Peter's anxiety considerably. Mr Hardy was then assertive enough to wield authority over Jane, who, finding her parents united, obeyed with some inner relief despite a continued show of adolescent defiance. The need for the adolescent to find his or her parents united against rivalrous intrusion is described more fully in Chapter 8 of *Adolescence and Breakdown.*

The shift in this family encounter, although apparently small, was important because, in the next family skirmish, Mr Hardy intervened decisively much earlier in the proceedings. In the final reckoning father's authority increased somewhat from its previous low ebb. The marriage revived, Jane became less out of control and Peter felt more secure.

How did the change effect each person's emotional development? Peter was able to identify with the more assertive quality in his father, and was able to experience anger and confrontation as potentially constructive instead of something so dangerously explosive that it had to be avoided at all costs. As her parents' interest in each other revived, Jane was under less pressure to keep both parents titillated with the idea of irresponsible sexuality. She was also more able to identify with the caring domestic qualities of her mother; she had brought herself to do the washing-up. The development turmoil produced by adolescence also throws parents into the melting pot. The family dragged Mr Hardy through the barrier which repudiated all anger, including its assertive qualities. Mrs Hardy was no longer called upon to be the dragon behind the family rules, could feel more valued as a wife and mother; no longer just a ferocious cook unappreciated except at each ritual handing in of her notice. Mandy sat taking it all in. Her active fantasy life, conscious and unconscious, was fed by the open threats of desertion and warnings about death. The family-repudiated themes, and their defences against them, were being passed on to the next generation. What she will do with them is a story for the future.

Adolescents' Challenge to Family Myths

The Hardy family mythology—their joint view of themselves which hid repudiated themes—emerged, after this period, somewhat more secure with only slight modifications. This mutually accepted view had been of a 'united family, with a mother who was a good cook, caring well for her family, lovingly supported by a father who was competent and never angry'. The repudiated theme—a taboo nightmare-drama flowing in the opposite direction—was of parents unfaithful to each other with mother murderously angry and father violent and incompetent: the whole family dangerously battling together, leading to a break-up, perhaps on Oedipal lines, i.e. Jane living with father, Peter with mother. It will be obvious to the reader that by and large these family value-systems also reflect society's attitudes: the two sets of myth-ology—family and cultural—interweaving with each other.

Adolescents can often see through the veneer of the family myth to spot the potential for avoided dramas. Jane, in particular, challenged the preferred image and brought the avoided themes closer to the surface. In that testing situation her parents did not do irrevocable battle, and father showed some capacity (small in an outsider's view but large in the family's eyes) to be firm. The fear of a calamitous outcome following angry confrontations was somewhat defused. Henceforth the defence was less brittle: now less of a myth, more of a reality. This reduction in polarisation between myth and disowned themes is important. The adolescent is capable of identifying with either set of values, often choosing those which seem most genuine. Adolescents may select the family's 'anti-value' system as opposed to a false façade. In doing so, they may then be used as the exception which proves the rule; 'We are a united family, except for. . . .'

For sake of argument the outcome in the Hardy family might have been less satisfactory. Jane might have become permanently labelled in a new family myth, as 'the problem' who somehow contained within her *all* the repudiated irresponsible sexuality and anger. A pregnancy might have provided the kernel of a suitably dramatic family legend that would focus the taboo feelings on Jane and provide a cautionary tale for posterity. Alternatively, father might have become the scapegoat by being labelled 'depressed'.

In many families, of course, a move towards less rather than more control over the adolescent is the healthy change. Society's present-day emphasis on freedom for its adolescents would harmonise with a shift in that direction. Jane brought back stories of her friends' extreme freedom. For the Hardy's the move towards more adequate control was achieved with dissonance (literally!)

Change is, of course, not confined to scenes. Family myths —and the repudiated themes that they hide and control— develop, crystallise or fade over the history of a family, with all its events, crises, additions and separations. In Chapter 8 of *Adolescence and Breakdown* the course of a second family's mythology is described, tracing its course from marriage until the 'problem child' brings the family to treatment. In the second part of this chapter we shall move on to look at the way in which the inner world of the family with all its drama interlocks with the wider social *milieu*.

The Family in Society

Most of us are brought up in a family, live our adult lives in a family and may, if we are lucky, die in a family. Whether we are as young as Mandy, or as old as Mrs Green, the family is our main source of love and nurture, fulfilling biological and psychological needs. But the family also pro-

E

vides a model experience that influences the nature of all our other relationships, and in so doing, fulfils certain functions for the society of which it is a part. Whilst these functions are primarily educative, to do with passing on a way of life and set of values, they are also economic. The family organises and provides human resources on which the wider system depends, and it provides them in accordance with certain mores and conventions.

There is a constant flow or interchange between individual family culture and the collection of ideas, values and practices that make up the wider culture. Although every family is unique, its members internalise and conform to values that are widely held. If they deviate from these in certain basic areas, the law of the land will impose limits and sanctions. At the same time, law is man-made and is slowly but constantly changed to reflect changes in social attitudes about what is considered to be deviant behaviour. Thus each family influences the values and beliefs which become institutionalised and part of conventional behaviour, and is in turn influenced by them, in a kind of reciprocal relationship.

Problems can, however, be institutionalised in the same way as positive values (Miller[4]). The difficulty is that attempts to find a starting point of individual, family or social problems can follow a never-ending 'chicken and egg' pattern, and the most we can do is to keep all three constantly in mind. David Cooper[5] attempts to do this in a revolutionary critique of the family. He extends the idea of the family's socialising function beyond necessary moral standards and the incest taboo, to excessive prohibition. He believes that instinctual control is emphasised at the expense of valuable expression of feeling, particularly of tenderness. His thesis raises far-reaching issues questioning the validity or desirability of the family as a social unit. Although beyond the scope of this chapter, such issues alert us to the fundamental assumptions on which our approach to the family is based and which underlie the tradition of adolescence in the family as a time of crisis.

66

The Hardy Family in Their Social Environment

Adolescents in their challenge to established family culture are a vital source of new possibilities. The effect of improved educational facilities and rapid technological development has in some ways loosened traditional family ties. But it is often the adolescent's boundless hunger for new experience that brings the real impact of innovation into the family with a variety of interest, activities and life-styles. Opportunities for travel and for exploration through the intellect and senses are greater than ever before. But whilst the originality of adolescents can provide the family with a source of enrichment and growth, it can also be experienced as a threatening intrusion which must be defended against. This seems to be partly the case in the Hardy family.

Mr and Mrs Hardy find it difficult to understand, let alone share, Jane's passion for the strange electronic sounds of her stereophonic record-player. Mr Hardy cannot discuss Peter's experiences in the chemistry laboratory, or hardly know if they are true. The family cannot fully know the experiences and way of life that awaits Mandy when she reaches adolescence and beyond. Almost certainly, she will face the problems and the privileges of a greater choice of opportunity than Peter and Jane, and will become the target of the 'pop' market at an even earlier age. It is no longer a mere flight of fantasy to say that she might even go to the moon. The contrast between that possibility and the fact that her grandmother, Mrs Green, living in the same house, travelled in a horse-drawn carriage, and can remember the very first films and aeroplanes, is a striking indication of the span of experience and possibility contained within one family unit. This is the kind of picture, at the level of the individual family, which collectively provides the basis and possibility of ever-increasing social change. Social mobility is not only mobility of people, it is mobility of ideas and knowledge.

Technological change may offer the family this range of experience but it has also damaged the conditions in which biological life takes place. However, the basic *animal* nature of human beings remains, and changes very slowly, if at all,

67

producing a certain tension, with our sophisticated urban life-style. Living in a family is the way our essentially animal instincts are able to be expressed and enjoyed, but also controlled, as Cooper emphasises. Mandy climbs on her father's lap as the anxiety and excitement about a family battle for power and leadership takes place, like a young animal seeking protection, but watching and learning from the rest of the pack. Jane, like many girls of her age, feels unable to seek this closeness from her father. As an adolescent, she is sexually mature in her body, if not in her mind, and is expected increasingly to seek her physical closeness outside the family. Yet she must retain a substantial part of her emotional and economic dependence on the family until she herself marries. Her music is left alive in the room when she leaves as a symbolic indication of her need to be noticed, and to invite her father's curiosity into the primitive sounds and rhythm of her own person. She has learnt to express these needs in symbolic form, as an essential part of the family socialisation process, that prepares her for adult life in society.

Why Adolescence Becomes a Time of Crisis

The problem for Jane and Peter is that adolescence *becomes* a crisis because of the clash between what is happening to them in their animal bodies, and the kind of behaviour demanded of them as social beings by their family and wider social environment. The explosive fantasies embodied in Peter's tale of the chemistry experiment, and the explosive sounds of Jane's music, reflect not only their psychic state, but also the explosive body-state which underlies it. Adolescents are exploding with sexuality and sexual curiosity, and with animal aggression that is a necessary accompaniment to the animal's need to seek a mate, and for survival. Peter and Jane use the chemistry experiment and record-player—phenomena of a technological age—in the service of primitive biological expression. The question is whether their natural explosiveness is perpetuated by a social structure

68

which is itself a product of that same age—the nuclear family.

Social mobility has eroded the multigenerational extended family with its aunts, uncles, cousins, grandparents, and other close neighbourhood ties. People move to better climates or working conditions. Mrs Hardy's brothers, for example, had left her behind with few other relatives whilst they travelled the world. The smaller, tighter, unit of the nuclear family remains to meet almost all of each other's needs. Family ties between parent and child are often intensified with fewer relatives for either to turn to. Mrs Hardy was called upon to fill all the gaps left by her brothers. She in turn made greater demands on her husband, Jane and Peter, than if she had had the emotional support of the large family in which she grew up. The pressures are multiplied at Jane and Peter's adolescence when the parent-child bond has to change to enable all to move towards a more independent existence. The sexual and aggressive feelings, and their concomitant psychic stress which Jane and Peter experience as a result of body changes, thus take place within the context of intensely interdependent family relationships, and a history of emotional and physical closeness confined to parents and each other.

Adolescence can therefore become a more radical experience for parent and child than in earlier generations. There is a strange paradox between the variety of life-style put before Jane and Peter at school or on television, and the limits of intimate, personal experience imposed by being cuddled by fewer aunts, uncles and grandparents, or bathed and fed with fewer brothers, sisters, neighbours or cousins. The opportunities of the permissive age pull one way, whilst an inadequate repertoire of inner emotional experience can pull another. Peter turns to his books as a way of coping, but Jane seems in danger of floundering without a compass in a sea of conflicting currents.

Adolescents need transitional experiences *outside* of the family that will help them to discover and establish their separate identities. There is a link here with the boom in the commercial teenage market: records, pop-stars, fashions, fads. It is not only that the money is there, or the technology is there, *it is that the need is there*. Because adolescents have an ever-changing need, they are an ever-changing market. Jane and Peter's transition from child to adult requires experimentation with transitional roles, ideas, modes, and feelings. The confines of the small nuclear family, and the absence of extended family or long-standing neighbourhood relationships means that these transitional experiences have now more than ever to be sought and provided outside of the family, and yet without the long-term commitment of more permanent relationships. Here the reciprocity between family and wider society is exemplified. One could say on the positive side that the 'pop' market entrepreneurs fulfil a creative and socially necessary role, helping adolescents to develop. The need to feel and experiment with her body-image has, for example, led Jane Hardy willingly through a variety of hairstyles and fashions, a variety of dances and rhythms, and therefore of music-forms. A new film can lead to a new look and a new sound, a new, but transient, life-style for the adolescent hungry for fresh but uncommitted experience. On the negative side the pop world is impersonal and the orgies of emotion it offers, do not take place within the context of a relationship. The much idolised and imitated stars of the pop world do not always behave with the degree of responsibility that vulnerable adolescents need.

The spotlight of interest and publicity is undoubtedly on the adolescent. Maximum hope and possibility faces Jane and Peter at a time when their parents, in sharp contrast, face the harsh realities of middle-life (Jacques[6]). There is an unfortunate coincidence of the waxing of one generation with the waning of another. For example, Jane's sexuality flowers, as her mother faces the menopause, and the natural rivalry between mother and daughter can be turned into a bitter and envious struggle. The death of old Mr Green, after Mandy's birth, warned Mr and Mrs Hardy of the nearness of old age and of their own mortality. Peter's enthusiastic studying reminds both parents of the educational opportunities they had to forego in the interests of child-rearing. Although these are normal problems to be found in any family, they are also the material that feeds the struggle and conflict between the generations, and on which more serious difficulties are often based.

The consumer market feeds into these difficulties. Just as more and more investment goes into the teenage market, and social services for adolescents, so the excitement and novelty of the post-war boom in household consumer goods diminishes. Washing-machines and television sets have lost their status of luxury goods and become a customary part of everyday life. Recent television commercials include zany plugs for the latest 'pop' record, whilst adverts for washing powders and toilet soap seem repetitive and dull in comparison. In education too, attention to the forty-year-olds is only just beginning to come into its own with expansion in evening education and The Open University, but it has been and still is a slow process. The potential contribution of the forty-year-old to society may not necessarily be so much less than that of the adolescent, but *it is seen as less*. This gives many parents a feeling of being robbed of their own life and youth, at a time when they still feel potentially lively and youthful.

The disparity between the attention paid by society to the adolescent and to those in middle-life, perpetuates the conflicts and tensions of the 'generation gap'. Jane and Peter Hardy latch on to what outside society has to offer by way of aspirations, interests and activities. They are faced with important decisions regarding their career and future life. These can take them away from their family of origin or keep them closer to it. They can use the wide variety of roles offered by society as opportunities to achieve the kind of distance that they need in order to develop as separate individuals. But these 'opportunities' also have a momentum of their own, propelled emotionally and physically by changes from within and socially from without. Mr and Mrs Hardy do not share this process, although they may be stimulated by its effect on their son and daughter. The result may be some form of fruitful exchange, a collision or a drifting apart, which can lead to greater estrangement than adolescent or parent might have envisaged, from the tightness of the bonds created in their earlier shared life together. More often the family may experience the struggle as challenging and enriching, bringing each family member new experiences of himself and others.

REFERENCES

1. H. V. Dicks, *Marital Tensions* (London, Routledge & Kegan Paul, 1967).
2. A. J. Ferreira, 'Family Myth and Homeostasis', *Archives of General Psychiatry*, Vol. 9 (1963), pp. 457–63.
3. J. Byng-Hall, 'Family Myths Used as Defence in Conjoint Family Therapy', *British Journal of Medical Psychology*, Vol. 46 (1973), p. 239.
4. M. J. Miller, 'Residential Care: Some Thoughts and Speculations on the Literature', *Social Work Today*, Vol 5, No. 9 (1974).
5. D. Cooper, *The Death of the Family* (Harmondsworth, Penguin Books, 1972).
6. E. Jaques, 'Death and the Mid-Life Crisis', *International Journal of Psychoanalysis*, Vol. 46, Part 4 (1965).

5

Adolescence and Authority

MARILYN J. MILLER

Introduction

The adolescent is faced with a complex ever-extending world
of infinite opportunities and attitudes. This can be an exciting experience of instinctual and intellectual exploration, but
it can also be confusing and even frightening. Sometimes
impulses and fantasies threaten to get out of control. Choices
have to be made and limits have to be set. The younger
adolescent may not be able to do this for himself. He needs
the support of knowing that there is someone to whom he
can turn at times when he feels overwhelmed. At other times,
he needs to be left to struggle with his uncertainty about who
he is and what he can or should do: to explore and experiment with different aspects of himself and the outside world.
This poses difficulties: if the adults behave inconsistently,
adolescents can become bewildered, yet there must be
enough flexibility to allow the adolescent room for growth
and self-discovery. Hence the conflict between adolescents
and adults, their traditions and institutions is in part because
the balance between control and flexibility can never be just
right.

Interactions with Authority: Benign and Vicious Cycles

Authority is usually taken to mean the right to enforce

73

obedience or exert control. This raises the question of what it is that has to be controlled? Later a distinction will be made between *social* or *external* forms of authority and *inner* authority, although both involve a similar struggle; a struggle about the extent to which behaviour rooted in powerful and primitive instincts should be expressed or controlled, and in what ways. The interaction between authority and instinctual pressure within society and the individual, is a continuous cyclical process. The quality of the cycle can vary from relatively benign to vicious and mutually escalating. When the cycle becomes vicious, polarisation occurs in which extreme positions are taken, authority becoming primitive and denying all possibility of gratification or compromise, thus promoting primitive rebellion. Social authority juggles with the polarities of anarchy and fascism, whilst inner authority must avoid instinctual chaos without being unduly prohibitive.

The Adolescent Need for Confrontation

Society and individuals generally seek to avoid extreme positions whilst adolescents seem to seek them out in periodic confrontations with authority which form a *necessary* part of the *normal* developmental process. These confrontations involve authority figures in a continuous struggle to avoid the vicious cycle and to find an optimum balance of control and flexibility.

Confrontation between adult and adolescent is, however, pervaded by *fantasy* on both sides. Adolescents may fear that if their challenges are not successfully met and contained, murder will result. Winnicott[1] points out that the very act of growing up can be thought of by the adolescent as a killing off and supplanting of parental figures. Parents may fear that overt confrontation with adolescents will inevitably turn into a vicious, escalating experience. If the murderous fantasies of adolescents are confirmed by parents' fears in this way, the maturation process of adolescence can be inhibited.

Adolescents need confrontations in order to consolidate

the sense of inner authority developed in infancy. Between the ages of twelve and eighteen fundamental changes take place in the adolescent's responsibilities, which involve a shift from considerable dependence on external authority to relatively autonomous behaviour. The twelve-year-old may exercise responsibility in certain school or family duties, but the eighteen-year-old may be married, have a family of his own, can vote and is regarded as a responsible adult by the law of the land. This rapid shift in role and relationships requires much experimentation on the part of the adolescent, and a flexibility and generosity on the part of those around him, particularly those in his immediate family. Their values and attitudes will be most under fire.

In the many situations that involve adolescents in one way or another in relationships with authority, the nature of *inner* authority and the attitude towards *social* authority are intimately linked.

Piaget,[2] by systematically observing children of different ages playing in a game of marbles, demonstrates the development of inner authority in terms of intellectual understanding and emotional control. Before the age of four, he found that children seem only able to play individually. Between the ages of four and six they play together, but without awareness of real co-operation. Between seven and ten, they begin to co-operate, although often lacking a true understanding of the rules. By eleven or twelve years of age, they not only understand the rules, but feel sufficient mastery of the situation to change or modify them as desired. That is to say, they understand external authority and have sufficient sense of the possibilities of their own inner authority to be able to challenge an external situation with their own alternatives.

'Standing Alone'

Young adolescents are not only capable of challenging authority, they need at times to take a defiant stance that will leave them relatively unsupported and *standing alone* in the family. These experiences help them to explore, test and

75

gradually extend their own resources. Confrontations of this kind build up an inner repertoire of 'standing alone' experiences that facilitate the necessary shift from dependence on external authority to autonomous behaviour.

> For example, Paul, aged fifteen, was bored by his parents' avid interest in television and expressed his boredom in jeers and mockery that made family viewing impossible. He ignored his mother's whining conciliations—'The programme finishes soon, dear. Wait a little longer can't you?' —and continued his attack until father, who had been trying to keep out of the conflict, finally exploded, 'Get upstairs and leave us in peace. I've had enough of your cheek. You're getting too big for your boots.' Paul, somewhat surprised at the unusual strength of his father's feeling, stood up and concealed his reaction with a parting remark, 'I wonder where I get that from!' He went to his room and once inside relaxed the bold front and shivered a little with the cold as he looked around for something to do. He found nothing to interest him and finally drew his curtains aside, looking out at a view of the city lights twinkling an invitation. He fantasised slipping out of the house without his parents' knowledge, but then thought miserably of the few coppers in his pocket. He turned away, closed the curtains and stretched out on the bed, first admiring his changing physique and finally curling up and falling asleep.

Standing alone can, however, be a risky business, and there are a number of characteristically adolescent ways of coping with the stress and strains. Outside of the family, adolescents find their own supportive network in which various experiences of 'standing alone' in the family can be shared, exchanged and built up. These networks are often a peer group at school or in the neighbourhood.

> The next day Paul met his mates at school and boasted about the confrontation with his father, embellishing it as he went along. ' "Get upstairs," he said, so I sat there. He didn't know what to do. I'll take him on properly one of

these days [clenching a fist and shaking it], then he'll really be in trouble. I told him to keep his rotten programme. I had better things to do'.

Although there are no strict patterns, girls and boys tend to establish slightly different support systems. Girls may form into small groups or more often rely on the confidence of one or two special friends, whilst boys, more intent on displays of strength and power, tend to stick to the group or the gang, and to shun the need for special friends as a sign of weakness or homosexuality. Some adolescents find the competition of both family and peer group too fierce and may withdraw and explore their experience of 'standing alone' in more complete isolation.

> Ruth, aged sixteen, was a slight, pretty girl who was out-going as a child, with many friends. At puberty she began to feel left out as her friends' conversations turned away from walking and horse-riding, and on to clothes and pop-music and the boys on the bus going home. She felt embarrassed that her body was developing so much more slowly than the other girls, and would rush out from school at four o'clock to catch an earlier bus. When she arrived home she ignored her mother's usual enquiry about the day—'Leave me alone, I've got some work to do.' 'Well, at least have some tea before you start. You spend so much time with your books.' 'I'll get my own.' 'But Ruth. . . .' 'I'll get my own.' She disappeared upstairs.

Confrontation often takes place over behaviour that draws attention to the rapid bodily changes taking place in the adolescent. Increasing physical strength is often a preoccupation of teenage boys and frequently emerges in confrontations between father and son, but also between older brothers and contemporaries. A rough and tumble with an older and stronger boy can often be a safe and valuable way of testing new found physical strength. Challenge and explosiveness can thus be expressed without much damage and inner anxieties about murderous potential can be allayed by an experience of containment.

77

Where containment is not experienced, and the young adolescent becomes precociously strong, his inner omnipotent fantasies are confirmed and he may feel that his thoughts and his body are getting out of control. This can lead to a situation of local notoriety where an adolescent is often given a nick-name, such as 'Big John', which he can in part enjoy, but inside he may feel lonely and destructive and unable to experience the warm, loving side of relationships.

The Kray twins[3] are an extreme example of this kind of development with their legendary neighbourhood supremacy at the age of sixteen. Although their subsequent career of violence and crime could be seen, in terms of the values of the criminal world, as a relatively successful one, both experienced periods of extreme loneliness and misery in which their only bonds were with mother and each other. For one of them, at times, even this broke down and his view of the world became totally paranoid and delusory. Otherwise their lives became a never-ending search for admiration from higher and higher authorities in the criminal world to provide some feeling of not entirely 'standing alone', and some substitute for the love that is an important part of more personal confrontations.

The confrontation with authority that draws attention to physical strength is also a statement about sexuality. For boys this is often an *underlying* statement: I can take you on any day (and that means I could claim your woman if I chose too). The direct expression of sexuality to mothers and girl-friends does take place, but is at first less important in itself than as currency in the male potency struggles of the peer group. In later adolescence, when the feeling of physical potency has been securely tested and retested in rivalries with other males, it becomes safe enough to be expressed sexually in a more genuinely heterosexual context.

Girls, on the other hand, often select sexual behaviour as the main arena of confrontation from early adolescence onwards. In Chapter 4, where the Hardy family are described, Jane invites parental anxiety and curiosity about her sexuality by staying out excessively late on Saturday night. She came down to the family's Sunday lunch, provocatively clothed in a dressing-gown that revealed her well-developed body, and reactivated the previous night's fantasies and anxieties about her sexual behaviour. Similarly:

> Valerie, just thirteen, was regarded as a brilliant girl with a good chance of going on from grammar school to university. She worked hard and diligently. One day her English teacher noticed that Valerie had a sheet of scribbled paper jutting out beneath her exercise book. 'What's that?' she asked. Valerie tried to conceal it, 'Nothing—just rough paper.' 'Let me see?' Reluctantly Valerie handed over a sheaf of notes as the friend beside her looked on with dismay. At a glance the teacher could see that the notes were an account of a fantasised romantic involvement between herself and one of the senior girls. 'This is disgusting', she said. 'Where on earth did you get these ideas? This is obscene. You will discuss the whole matter with the headmistress.' Valerie said nothing but looked hurt and miserable. What had seemed like an amusing joke between her and her friend now felt like a wilful, obscene attack on her favourite teacher. It seemed as if their good relationship might never be repaired, and she felt overwhelmed by shame and disgust at what she had done.

In this latter example, the teacher reacted to Valerie's sexual fantasies and confusion in a primitive and escalating way. What might have been an opportunity for understanding and explanation became a vicious cycle from which Valerie internalised a primitive, frightening experience that made it more difficult for her to bring out her sexual anxieties in future.

Girls need a response to their sexuality that will help them to feel that sexual development is a good thing. Menstruation and breast development may at first be uncomfortable and painful, even when eagerly awaited. Confrontation within the family over late hours and modes of dress are some of the ways of trying to express confusion and anxiety. Girls need to evoke a parental reaction that both recognises the fact of sexual development and provides some kind of benevolent understanding and control. In particular, the teenage girl needs to arouse *paternal* interest and awareness of her sexuality and it becomes crucial that mothers do not react as if this were the serious sexual threat of another woman. Daughters need to feel that mothers can allow them their sexuality and help them with all their anxieties and confusions. Where the relationship between daughter and mother is exclusively one of confrontation, something is going wrong. Often it may be that mother's own sexuality is insecure, and she therefore has to block the contact between father and daughter to reduce the threat of being supplanted in his affections.

Another familiar way in which adolescents provoke and confront authority figures is with deafeningly loud and strangely primitive 'pop' music. This can be used to tantalise parents and to display to them the mysteries and uniqueness of the adolescent experience. For boy and girl alike it can also be a comforting and stimulating external expression of the mysteries of their inner experience of change. Other areas of challenge assert the adolescent's exploration and growing sense of his own identity: wearing clothes which challenge established family culture; exploring extreme or bizarre political or religious beliefs and going through radical changes of habit, such as eating strange foods and sleeping new hours. These are not instances of rebellion for rebellion's sake, but parts of the essential experience of 'standing alone' required to establish a sound identity.

The Impact of Adolescent Challenge of Parental Roles

In adolescent confrontations with parental authority, I believe the role of father is vital to the family. Parents can only respond with generosity and sensitivity to the often vicious challenge of adolescents when they feel relatively secure themselves. In some families, fathers make a less direct contribution to *child*-rearing than they need to make at *adolescence*. Mothers can absorb and manage the impact of young children more easily than the impact of teenagers who become larger and more challenging with every month that passes. Mothers need to feel sufficiently supported and appreciated by fathers to cope with the diminishing dependency of children and frequent attacks on mothering. The prospect of children leaving home often involves a far greater adjustment in role for mother than for father since she is often used to a daily routine in which child-minding has been a central feature. She may not, for example, have gone out to work while the children were growing up. Deficiencies in the marital relationship may have been made up for by the rewards of motherhood and the presence of children. These, and many other factors, put mothers in a particularly vulnerable position when children reach adolescence. In addition, as has already been pointed out, adolescent boys need direct confrontations and acceptance by fathers, and girls need *paternal* appreciation before they can feel truly feminine. So at adolescence, fathers are required more than ever to support mothers and bear more directly the brunt of family demands. Adolescents need to feel their primitive feelings can be explored, expressed and contained by parents who feel relatively secure with their own aggression and sexuality.

Patterns of Challenge: Antecedents of the Benign and Vicious Cycles

Patterns of challenge vary in accordance with each individual's *infantile* experience of parental authority. There is a continual cycle of projection and introjection that goes on within the family, and this is heightened by the biological and psychological pressures of adolescent development. The balance of control and flexibility within this cycle, that is, within and between individuals, can never be just right. However, early experiences determine how far confrontation is likely to be experienced as benevolent and growth-producing or vicious and mutually escalating.

The adolescent's capacity to negotiate and cope with the multitude of pressures and opportunities that confront him

81

in everyday life, depends on the inner pattern of values and relationships which have been built up over the years: what it means to him to question or challenge parental authority; what are the expected repercussions of disagreeing or disobeying? In other words, *what is the nature and quality of the internalised relationship between impulse and authority?* What is the pattern of coping with an internal conflict between wanting to do one thing, and feeling he ought, or is being requested, to do another?

Infants rely on parents for instinctual gratification: feeding, cleaning, cuddling, and at times being left to cry. The infant is preoccupied with his own and his mother's body and the quality of this early physical and psychological intimacy plays an important part in determining the harmony or conflict in later life, between sexual and aggressive impulses and their control or expression in social relationships. The infantile experience of the boundaries and quality of gratification and frustration becomes internalised, forming an inner pattern of wishes and anticipated responses that are confirmed or repudiated by later experience. Freud and others after him, notably Ferenczi, Abraham and Klein elaborated upon the relationship between bodily experiences and mental development. Although there is varying emphasis on the influence of oral, anal and genital experiences, it can be assumed that all play their part.

J. C. Flugel[4] describes an ideal to be aimed for in human relationships in his notion of a 'spontaneity of goodness'. This involves a full harmonious interaction between instinctual impulses and the sense of responsibility and control that can be called inner authority. Such harmony requires a maturity within and between individuals, that will permit co-operation based on mutual respect. But most of us achieve such harmony, at best, only part of the time, whilst at other times a more primitive interaction takes place. There are remnants of suspicion, fear, defiance, feelings of having submitted to authority, or a more general wariness.

Adorno *et al*[5] found that children of authoritarian, controlling, exploitative parents tend to reproduce this early relationship in all facets of their later life: marriage, religion, and social and political attitudes. The infant's fear and admiration of the power-orientated parent leads to a later clinging to strong and often prejudiced views: a tendency to see things in terms of black and white, and to be unable to appreciate alternative outlooks, compromise or subtlety. The lives of such individuals seemed geared to warding off feelings, ideas and attitudes which are seen as 'bad', 'weak' or 'forbidden'. These attitudes are then projected on to other persons, groups or races, and subjected to harsh and even sadistic criticism. Alternatively, the individual may be given to indulging in occasional bursts of 'forbidden' activity, often of a sexual or sadistic kind, only to suffer extreme self-recrimination after the event. The authors describe this pattern of living as based on an essentially dichotomous view of the self and the world into good and bad, black and white. Such rigidity deprives the individual of the pleasure of developing a multifaceted existence fully and freely, and inhibits creative potential.

Rycroft[6] elaborates the ideas of Freud and other authors by making a distinction between internalisation of authority based on *love,* and internalisation based on *fear.* He points out that internal authority tends to be of an absolute nature, being developed in infancy when it is usual to think absolutely. But internalisation based on fear leads to intense conflict later, in making choices and decisions between different ideas or courses of action. Fear may promote a need to agree or submit passively to authority outwardly, whilst inwardly breeding envy and defiance. The individual can become caught between fear and defiance, and suffer excessive guilt whatever course of action is chosen. This dilemma may be resolved by slumping into inertia and failing to achieve, or by expressing conflict in obsessional symptoms. Outwardly conforming adolescents are often holding resentment akin to that expressed by their rebellious peers, inside themselves. This is sometimes manifested in outward behaviour, by a repeated spoiling of whatever achievement or course of action is pursued. For example, there is the brilliant child who studies hard at school, including during adolescence, fulfilling ambitions, and providing a source of pride for his parents. He does well for the first year of university, and then surprises everyone by losing interest in his academic work, and taking up with an extremist group, which rejects the values to which he had so rigorously adhered. This is a belated explosion of resentment towards, not only the external authority of parents and society, but also towards his own inner authority to which he has hitherto been a slave. The sudden rebellion may provide a temporary diversion, and an opportunity for enrichment and integration, or the basic conflict may remain the same, and can lead to an erratic pattern of rebellion and conformity. This pattern is extremely frustrating and distressing, not only to the adolescent, but also to those around him.

Rycroft points out that it is quite healthy and normal for the adolescent to experience *some* guilt and conflict in the course of exploration outside his own family. But he distinguishes between this and the extreme guilt induced by fear, which leads to a restricted experience in adolescence, and neurotic symptoms, or a belated rebellion at the cost of hard won achievements.

Adolescence and Social Authority

Moving on to 'social authority', one can see similarities between the description of family patterns and the cyclical processes that take place between institutionalised forms of social control (fulfilling a parental role) and the pressures for social change (fulfilling the role of adolescent challenge). The difference, as Susan Holland points out in her chapter, is that at this level challenge comes from a variety of social groups and from people of all ages. Nevertheless, the part played by adolescents themselves in these processes still deserves consideration. Their role seems to have changed significantly, in a way that adds an important perspective to the topic of adolescence and authority.

As with individuals and families, inner authority is a means of controlling and mediating primitive instinctual impulses, so in wider society, an institutionalised system of authority is a means of implementing and preserving basic

84

values and standards of civilised behaviour. This social authority is symbolised by various rules, regulations, procedures, uniforms and so on, and is most evident in the law of the land and the parliamentary system. But social authority, like parental authority, can be wielded in different ways.

Our literature reflects the anxiety in society about the more primitive forces taking over, typified perhaps in Orwell's *1984* and seen as inevitable in the same author's *Animal Farm.* Such writings as these go together with phrases like 'power tends to corrupt, and absolute power tends to corrupt absolutely'. They reflect anxiety that primitive instincts might become unleashed and masquerade under the guise of social authority or usurp the more benevolent forms of social control. The historical reality of nations at war and in states of revolution bears witness to this possibility. However much we aim for the ideal of co-operative relationships based on mutual respect, we also respond to the more primitive potentialities of power. Even though our response may contain adult echoes of childhood fears and suspicion, it may also be appropriately cautious. Just as exchanges within the family can take on a primitive, persecuting quality, so social authority can sometimes lose touch with the very values it purports to uphold.

Weber[7] distinguished between three different types of social authority which still seem apt: the legal, traditional and charismatic. In this country parliamentary rule, and with it the development of a sophisticated legal system, established the domination of 'legal' and 'traditional' styles of authority. Although the practice and policies of our social institutions are designed to reflect gradual changes in custom and belief, the problem lies in the fact that *social institutions change slowly.*

Bureaucracy takes on an almost Kafkaesque quality whilst social change accelerates as a result of developments in technology and education. The pressure for change has thus begun to overtake and outweigh the institutional means for responding.

Just as threats evoke a defensive stance in individuals, so

they can in the way that social institutions operate. Emery and Trist[8] point out that changes in values and attitudes are required if institutions are to make the most of these pressures for change rather than suppress or fight with them. Otherwise a benign cycle of interaction between parent institutions and the continual generation of new ideas can become a persecutory one. Collaboration must replace competition here, just as in family relationships that come under pressure at adolescence.

> The violent confrontation in the USA between students and police on the Kent State campus is an example of the extremes to which this vicious circle can be taken. Students were shot, as subsequent reports show, unnecessarily. The police (parental) reaction became even more primitive than the student action that provoked it.

It seems as if the role of adolescents in relation to social authority is changing and that the traditional adolescent challenge may now have the support of a much wider section of society. It is here that improved education and the mass media play an important part in preparing the adolescents with a variety of life-styles and information. Reading, travelling and watching films have broken down many of the old national and local barriers previously imposed by wealth, class and opportunity. Add to this the energy and drive rooted in the physiological and psychological state of adolescents, and there is a combination which is both original and saucy enough to challenge long-standing patterns, and efficient enough to be valued by substantial numbers of the more reticent radicals. Thus today's adolescent carries not only the internal forces for challenge and growth that arise from his own biological state of development, but also some of the hopes and frustration of the older generation.

Adolescents are more informed and articulate than hitherto, and often offer answers as well as questions. The impact on the social system, has been strengthened by the fact that their intentions are not only personal, they can now be political. Thus returning to Weber's models, the preponderance of legal and traditional forms of authority in the context of increasing pressures for social change, has led to the emergence of charismatic leaders, some of whom are notable for their youth. Perhaps the most striking example is Bernadette Devlin, whose road to Parliament was that of a heroine with a strong body of disciples, whose differences could be sunk in their admiration and support of her. Northern Ireland clearly has not avoided the vicious persecuting cycle of Kent State, but even so their elect representative has participated in 'the system' with at least the possibility of a constructive exchange and without dialogue reaching total breakdown, as it did in Kent State. It is as if the climate of frustration is such that the way has been opened for those with the youth, hope and energy to *take on* an authority which hitherto was only theirs to challenge.

It could be said that this argument only applies to the middle-class educated adolescent, and so far as it pertains to highly articulate, political involvement, this may be true. But the same process takes place with a different style, at the more deprived end of the social scale. Skinheads and muggers (male or female) challenge laws and morality with a defiance and *pride* that has wider roots than in their individual psychology. It seems possible that there is an unconscious recognition on the part of the adolescent that he has the support or even *represents the feelings* of a portion of the older generation. There is a cultural equivalence between the student rebel who challenges the system, and the skinhead who makes a head-on collision with the law. *Student and skinhead speak not only for themselves.* Many adults are also disillusioned with the police force, the Church and the quality of life in general. The promised land of a wealthy industrial society, free from major wars and with the ideals that led to the creation of the welfare state has been a disappointment to many. They may not support violence and theft, in fact, they may express harsh criticism of the younger generation, but monotonous work, where the only excitement is in the next wage claim, or the shorter working week leads to violent sentiments and a desire to rob the 'haves' on behalf of the 'have nots'. The style of the adolescent is usually uncontrolled, but the style of the discontented adult is moving in the same direction with violent pickets, and other strong-arm tactics. The process of a student rebellion, a skinhead attack, an industrial dispute, is basically similar. It is a challenge, and at times an attack on the power of an authority, that is experienced as frustrating, greedy or untrustworthy. Or it may be an attempt to impose a violent power out of a sense of impotence, poverty and resentment. The important thing is that the challenge and attack are based on inner feelings, but enhanced and perpetuated by social group pressures, and the actual conditions of life.

Conclusion

It can therefore be said that *relationships with authority involve a balance between the drive to express and gratify instinctual impulses and the moral and social demands of the individual and his environment.* The point has already been made that a fully harmonious balance is difficult to achieve in adulthood. However, it is even more so in adolescence because of the special features of adolescent development. The adolescent *has* to find room for the expression of intense sexual and aggressive feeling in a way which is acceptable to himself, his family, and society as a whole. The speed of bodily change requires a speed of change in family and social relationships which is difficult for adults and adolescents, and inevitably causes tension and disruption in establishing relationships. Parents have to find new ways of responding to sexually aware offspring and facilitate their moves towards independence. The difficulty is that the intrinsic drive for rapid change in the adolescent is *not* matched by a corresponding drive in the parent for whom change is therefore more of a challenge. Similarly, at a societal level, education and technological change can throw a community into a state where the forces for social change outstrip the capacity of social institutions to respond. Just as parents of adolescents are often stretched to the limits of their originality and responsiveness so social authority needs new structures that allow room for continuous change and challenge.

REFERENCES

1. D. W. Winnicott, *Playing and Reality* (London, Tavistock, 1971).
2. J. Piaget, *The Moral Judgement of the Child* (London, Routledge & Kegan Paul, 1950).
3. J. Pearson, *The Profession of Violence – The Rise and Fall of the Kray Twins* (London, Weidenfeld & Nicolson, 1972).
4. J. C. Flugel, *Man, Morals and Society* (London, Duckworth, 1948).
5. T. W. Adorno, *et al.*, *The Authoritarian Personality*, Parts I and II (New York, Wiley, 1964).
6. C. Rycroft, *Anxiety and Neurosis* (London, Allen Lane, The Penguin Press, 1968).
7. M. Weber, 'The Three Types of Legitimate Rule', in A. Etzioni, *Complex Organisations: A Sociological Reader* (New York, Holt, Rinehart & Winston, 1961).
8. F. E. Emery and E. L. Trist. *Towards a Social Ecology: A Contextual Appreciation of the Future in the Present* (London, Plenum Press, 1972).

6

Adolescence and Sexuality

SIMON MEYERSON

> *Monty:* Answer for your love. Why does it not add up?
> *Woman:* Out of love there comes forth birth
> And out of birth there comes forth jealousy
> And out of jealousy there comes forth hate
> And out of hate there comes forth war
> And out of war there comes forth sadness
> And out of sadness there comes forth
> ... love. ... Love has such a strange
> method of mathematics.
> (Extract from the play *The Re-Enactment*)

Adolescent sexuality reveals a moving emotional kaleidoscope of colourful feelings and changes that can be exciting and frightening, pleasurable and painful, joyous and sad, loving and hating. It encompasses evolving experiences and interlinking relationships of others-to-self, self-to-self, self-to-others. Its spectrum stretches from virginal ignorance to full carnal knowledge, from the poignancy of utter loneliness or loving tenderness to the brutality of gang-bang violence.

The 'permissive society' always seems to be 'other people' *and* adolescents. The mass media seem always busy making capital of the alleged sexual excesses of adolescents, such as thirteen-year-old girls going in for second abortions; or

90

parents putting their daughters on the pill the moment menstruation begins; or depicting a sort of sexual Russian roulette where the modern adolescent daringly flirts with promiscuity, VD and pregnancy. Some observers are even asking 'Is ordinary sex enough?' suggesting that adolescents are becoming so blasé about sex that they crave the added 'kicks' of orgies, 'kinkiness', drugs. Publicity was recently given to dating habits of nine-year-old teeny-bopper Californians. And more recently of weeny-boppers.

The voyeuristic posture of older generations has the dynamic factor of causing exhibitionistic adolescents to go even daringly further than their 'square' forebears. But adolescent sexuality can be very deceptive for those looking on and seeing only the external glow of sex-appeal, youth, beauty, flamboyance, promiscuity and discotheque-like gyrations.

The conflicting reactions to sexuality in society are complicated enough for adults. How, then, can adolescents cope with the new and bewildering impulses circulating through their bloodstreams and their daydreams? Finding a *modus vivendi* to the painful and pleasurable enigmas of sexuality is one of the central paradoxes of adolescence, and of life itself.

Infantile Sexuality

I would like to refer to the work of a New York therapist, Elisabeth Fehr, who practices birth therapy. With the aid of Mrs Fehr as the mother and a team of helpers, the subject 'relives' his birth while pushing himself rhythmically along a thirty foot mattress. The actions and experiences involved in this 'birth' and 'post-birth' relationship are reported to have uncanny familiarity with the person's original birth experiences, both physically and emotionally. After witnessing many 'rebirths' and experiencing the 'rebirth' myself, I believe that the birth experience, the breaking of the biological link with the mother and the very first external reciprocal contacts between mother and child are important for later sexual relationships. Some subjects reported prenatal experiences such as feelings or 'memories' of parental intercourse

91

while they were still in the womb. The physical and emotional feelings between the parents during sexual contact also seem able to leave powerful physical and emotional memory imprints on the unborn child and may influence later sexuality.

Descriptions of infantile sexuality are well documented elsewhere. Here follow brief comments on the early psychosexual relationships. The mother can be both intimate and gratifying regarding oral and anal needs, desires and activities. But when the child makes demands for genital erotic desires to be gratified, the child is in for a shock and complexities arise as this area of erotic desire is additionally emotionally charged At its simplest, these desires form part of what Freud called the Oedipus complex with its attendant wishes and feared consequences, such as the castration complex which affects both boys and girls in different ways. The child's sexuality is abruptly confronted by a phenomenon peculiar to man—the incest taboo, which is a conglomerate of fear of retaliation from, and concern for, the parents. So great is the shock that the child's Oedipal sexuality goes into a phase of repression, the latency phase—another phenomenon peculiar to man and to which Freud attributes man's capacity for creating a higher civilisation, but also man's neurosis vulnerability.

Before discussing adolescent sexuality, it seems important to mention the parent-child capacity to play. Trust, joy, interpersonal good feelings and happiness evolve through play. Playing is another way of loving. It will certainly influence later sexuality, not only in foreplay, sex-play, the joy of sharing, giving and receiving, but also in the pleasurable interplay of fantasy and reality.

Adolescent Sexuality

Adolescent sexuality is like an evolving, complex, kaleidoscopic jig-saw or crossword puzzle in which the pieces, the clues, the questions, the struggles and explorations, and the answers may change shape and colour before the full pattern is formed. Changes in one area influence another. There are

causes and effects, actions and reactions, expected and unexpected. There are obsessions and digressions, progressions
and regressions. There are times of clarity and times of
obscurity; times of failure and of triumph; glow and
gloom. There are times of excesses and interactions; times
of stillness and reflection. Sexual feelings may arise, respond
and influence the gestalt in different ways at different
times.

Adolescence is a developmental phase in its own right. It
does not have to be totally dependent on the infantile past as
now there are greater autonomous physical, social and intellectual choice-making skills. For example, a boy, through his
parents' divorce, and living most of his life with no father
and hence weak in male identity, can introject into his
identity an admired teacher who can add structure to his
personality.

Blos[1] and others divide adolescence into three phases:
early, mid and late. This demarcation is followed here but it
should be underlined that adolescent sexuality is a highly
individual process. A patient put it like this, 'Take a class of
twenty-five boys aged fourteen: five will be playing around
sexually with girls; fifteen will still be goggle-eyed and playing with themselves; and five will still be playing with their
Meccano sets.' It is not unusual for late developers suddenly
to outstrip their peers in both physique and technique. Sometimes the precocious remain fixed in 'technique' or can even
regress; for example, a girl, precocious in sexual relationships with men and disappointed with her frigidity, regresses
to satisfying relationships with maternal women.

In order that adolescent sexuality may be fully and
healthily developed, a 'weaning' is required, a transition
from earlier bonds to new ones, earlier desires to new ones,
earlier means of gratification to new means and new ends.
One end not available in infantile sexuality was sexual intercourse. The child was excluded from that act of parental
sovereignty. But at adolescence somehow the tide turns. The
parental monopoly of sexual intercourse can be challenged
not just in fantasy but in reality. Whereas before the parents

93

looked after not only the body of the child but exerted some kind of control over his emotional and intellectual development and provided for almost all his needs, now changes in power, perspective and relationship occur. Now a private sexuality develops. These are areas of his life from which parents are excluded, and there is secrecy and outside sharing with peers and partners on an unprecedented scale. These are necessary steps in the struggle for private emotional territory and a sense of individuality. Sexuality has to be 'owned' by the adolescent and it has therefore to be explored by him with relative independence. Throwing it into the laps of parents, as with childhood feelings and problems, can cause complications. Sex is the adolescent's very own thing. The formula of pairing between self and parents has to be amended by both parents and adolescent although there are undoubtedly times when support and frank information are needed.

It would seem that to reach the capacity for mature loving heterosexual intercourse, the original dilemma presented by the Oedipus complex which was repressed in latency would have to be faced again. This time the solution to incest must not be repression but based on sublimation presumably, and on a capacity to find alternative healthy loving relationships outside the family. Refacing the Oedipal dilemma and going *through* it, i.e. like going through the eye of the tornado, makes adolescence and eventual non-incestuous heterosexual intercourse such a possibly turbulent time. Hence, adolescence has been described as 'going through the doldrums' (Winnicott) but at the same time is a second chance, an opportunity for a replay to evolve through Oedipal and pre-Oedipal disappointments and fixations.

With the resurgence of sexuality, propelled by physical and emotional changes, comes the resurgence of the exciting and frightening fantasies experienced at the Oedipal stage which culminated in repression. If the repression was caused primarily by fear of retaliation, *fear* will be a powerful accompaniment of sexual and erotic feelings now, or be instrumental in repressing or distorting them (e.g. giving sexuality an ingredient of revenge, sadism or masochism). If it was based also to a great degree on concern for the parents, the turbulence and fright component of adolescent sexuality can be less. What was experienced at the height of the Oedipal desires and fears, unless modified unconsciously during latency, is likely to reveal itself at adolescence.

Broadly speaking, and in oversimplified form, there appear to be five interdependent areas of development that are prominent in the efflorescent and convergent processes leading to mature loving heterosexual intercourse: (a) body, (b) fantasy, (c) emotions, feelings, (d) 'technique' or the 'mechanics' of sex, and (e) partner encounters and other changing interpersonal relationships, e.g. with parents.

Early Adolescence

Early adolescence is a time of extraordinarily rapid efflorescence and transformation. Together with bodily changes are changes in fantasy life: unrepression of infantile erotic fantasies occurs and new ones bubble forth uncontrollably. The bewildering experience *'What's happening to me?'* can lead to answers of great anticipation or profound panic. For example, one pubescent girl whose breasts are budding may joyously exaggerate them by means of handkerchiefs and a bra; another, terrified, may flatten her chest to ensure that neither she nor others notice her emerging sexuality.

Early adolescence involves the inner confrontation between powerful sexual feelings and the incompletely formed adult self-identity. There can be unpredictable bewildering contradictions of mood, impulse and resolution; for example, masturbating six times in a day and then resolving never to touch one's organ again; or great joy at sexual impulses followed by deep depression at having these impulses. Conscious resolutions can be contradicted by unconscious and biological impulses.

Masturbation is the main form of sexual outlet. Less so for girls. A boy can personalise his penis as a 'partner' or sex-object. A girl can sexualise and personalise her whole body as a love partner or sex-object. Boys do this too but can find greater focus of satisfaction in their penises. Girls thus seem to be able to move more quickly into being embraced bodily by others, while boys are still clinging to masturbation. Some girls try to resist female sexuality and its implications and go through a tomboy phase. This seems to have two predominant reasons: an attempt to deny 'castration' (and being penetrated) by carrying on as if she had a penis; familiarising herself with eventual 'having' of the penis in heterosexual intercourse.

In adolescence, turmoil and confusion about sexuality often cannot be taken directly to parents for help because of the struggles with shame, disgust, morality and guilts derived from conscious and unconscious incestuous wishes, but also because of the struggle to separate from the parents. The 'intimacy zone' of contact undergoes profound changes not only for the adolescent but also for the parents. A denial of change in this oversensitive 'intimacy zone' and 'carrying on as before' can lead to surprising flare-ups. For example, one frequently hears of a girl of twelve being regarded as an angel and suddenly (usually on her using lipstick, the emergence of breasts or the onset of periods) there occurs violent animosity and the adolescent daughter suddenly finds herself labelled with the screamed epithets of 'whore', 'slut', 'prostitute'. This occurs when the parents have, in their own anxiety, tried too long to deny the emerging adolescent sexual changes and wish to keep the status quo infant-parent way of relating.

At adolescence, a different kind of intimacy is needed by both parent and adolescent rather than a sudden withdrawal of love to be replaced by hurtful and hateful attack and counter-attack. Unconscious and overt reassurance from parents is important in adolescent sexual identity: father accepting daughter's femininity and mother overcoming envy with healthy identification or vicarious gratification. An example of failure was that of an attractive thirteen-year-old girl who was 'shunted off' to boarding school. The father had become panicky at the emergence of his daughter's sexual attractiveness and both parents were unable to cope. The father drove the daughter to a school in the country. On the way, her first menstrual period began. She told her father and asked him to stop the car. He was embarrassed and, in his anxiety, rejecting. A few months later the daughter began to run away from school; she would find older men and have promiscuous relationships. Eventually she appeared in court on a drug charge to 'embarrass' her father for rejecting her. Later she had an illegitimate child and eventually became a heroin addict. A further example: an intelligent twelve-year-old boy was referred by his mother for failure at school. Unconsciously she and the adolescent were anxious about his emerging sexuality and the shift in the mother-child bond. In therapy he anxiously disclosed that homosexual feelings and mutual masturbatory practices with other boys were being indulged in. He also was afraid of fantasising sexual intercourse, because of vagina dentata beliefs that the vagina would bite his penis off. With minimal psychotherapeutic help the boy progressed to heterosexual relationships and improved scholastic achievement.

At early adolescence there is usually a defensive polarisation of males and females into different groupings. Pairings here are usually defensive and supportive and of the same sex, and can help cope with the 'panics and mechanics' of sexuality, e.g. reassurance about self-image, 'sex-appeal', gossipy sharing of sex-lore. Girls can kiss, embrace, fondle one another imagining the partner as the 'forbidden' opposite sex. Boys may masturbate in pairs or groups or even mutually masturbate for reassurance about the opposite sex. These pairings and sharing can be important bridging factors. The first attempted partnerings are usually with self (e.g. masturbation), narcissistic, part-object (e.g. attracted by girl's breasts), or with someone representing an idealised parent, or elements of these. The parents are retained as a sort of base from which to try out other kinds of pairing possibilities, and when 'casualty' results the adolescent can regress to be looked after as a child.

The 'try-outs' in fantasy (e.g. fantasies of pregnancy and having a baby or love relationships with pop-idols) are

97

important and can help progression through the stages and the traversing of complicated and vulnerable areas. Unjealous parental help and understanding are important in the 'crush' stage.

Nowadays one hears that many early adolescents are experimenting with short-cuts to sexual intercourse. Even though early adolescents are physically capable and some do indulge, generally the unconscious memories of Oedipal fears inhibit this and in actual fact a fairly circuitous and more reassuring route is usually taken before sexual intercourse is achieved. If, as does happen, full intercourse is indulged in, it usually means that it has been achieved because of an unduly exaggerated single factor (of the five mentioned), e.g. purely by mechanical means, not accompanied with loving emotions and with a girl who is feeling idolising love for him. Short cuts to intercourse are not infrequently tried, but emotional immaturities may remain masked by the pseudo-sophistication of 'technique' confidence.

As long as no outside sexual partnering is evident and as long as the childlike dependent bonds continue and sexuality is still 'contained' in secrecy, masturbation or fantasy, then flare-ups with parents do not actually occur until later. The parental pressure to keep sexuality controlled plus the pull of the sexual partner or the peer group usually leads to confrontation in the family. Adolescents can sometimes split their own sexuality so as to enjoy infantile benefits and bonds within the family as well as to secretly indulge in 'adult' sexuality outside the family.

The early transition to pairings and partnering are very important and who one selects for help in this is very important for now the psychological and sexual needs of the partner come to the fore. This can lead to progress, or seduction into a solution that may not be desired. Who one pairs with 'for the first time' can leave a profound effect on one's sexual identity. Surrounding circumstances here can hold an influence almost as strong as infantile history, e.g. public school.

Mid Adolescence

In the shifting anagram of adolescent sexuality, this is usually a time of exploration, experimentation, of real as well as fantasised sex proper. From the bewildering experiences of early adolescence slowly evolves the wobbly security of partial knowledge. The adolescent wants to find out *'Who or what am I?'* Sexuality is the prism of identity. He explores himself through situations, learns more clearly who or what turns him on, whether he is heterosexual or homosexual, child or adult, masculine or feminine, active or passive; he comes to terms with or changes the balance of a multiplicity of emotional innuendos and ambiguities. In the complex human kaleidoscopic crossword or jig-saw puzzle of the now magic, now tragic, enigmas of love, sex and identity, of self and other, he seeks more real answers to the urgent question *'Where do I fit in?'* Mid-adolescence is the time for testing reality, the time for risking satisfactions and disappointments, where the security of the masturbatory fantasy conquests can be put to the test so that real confirmation or disillusionment can occur.

The aim is to break from the parents and to find one's own two-person relationship. Thus a new triangle may form (parents-adolescent-partner). Now long-repressed conflicts can be powerfully resuscitated, this time acted out in some form with powerful emotions (even 'negative') that help deflect away from the incest solution to 'refind' a relationship outside the family that can lead to sexual relationships. The politics of exclusion are powerful in this process: at the Oedipal stage the child capitulated sexually from the triangle to leave the parental twosome intact; at adolescence, the adolescent has to again capitulate from the parental twosome and find his own twosome outside the family. But now it is the parents who also have to capitulate and leave the adolescent twosome intact. This struggle with interferences of past bonds is central to the drama of adolescence and of sexuality. The strange, but not completely unexpected, fact is that often the deeper the past love between parent and adolescent the more painful and difficult it is to give up that

99

love without recrimination, envy and jealousy. And the deeper the past hate, the easier it is to use sexuality and partner selection as a means of retaliation for past hurts, neglects and 'betrayals'.

With the hopeful, and anxious, possibilities of hetero-sexual intercourse with a partner outside the family, the scene for the universal family psychodrama can be enacted. More likely it is also a re-enactment because the triangle of parent-adolescent-partner can resuscitate unresolved Oedipal adolescent and sexual conflicts not only of the adolescent but of the parents. A system of projections and counter-projections can arise for sorting-out, as adolescents feeling anxious about sexuality can displace problems away from the relationship with the partner on to the parents and parents can displace unresolved conflicts on to the adolescent and the partner.

Whereas new experiences outside the parental domain were more secretive in early adolescence, they can now more openly struggle with parental control, domination and 'ownership'. Confrontation between parent and child is likely to happen: how it does, and with what smoothness or disruption or mutual concern, is crucial, for with sexual and separation struggles at a height, the potential for displacement into acting-out is also high. Oedipal type re-enactments are possible and the jealousy, hurt and desire for retaliation for Oedipal 'defeat' experienced earlier needs to be over-come. But the re-enactment contains an added dimension—a form of Oedipal victory for the adolescent is now possible. For example, the daughter *can* be more sexually attractive than the mother in the father's eyes. Not unknown is the phenomenon of the reverse Oedipus complex, where the overt or unconscious sexual desires of the parent for the adolescent can arise. The healthy elements of this are where mutual sublimation allows the adolescent to feel a better sense of self-image and desirability. Otherwise the sexuality can be acted-out, usually with disastrous results. Or, too defensively repressed, can manifest itself under the guise of overt hostility or in parents stopping a girl having boy friends. Or, the exact opposite, allowing promiscuity outside and so deflect the 'bad' sexuality on to the adolescent. It can lead to acts of repression or exaggeration by both parents and adolescents. It is not uncommon for parents' mid-life identity crises to be triggered off by or coincide with the crises of mid-adolescent sexuality.

Sexuality and identity become almost synonymous, and now is the time for a confirmation of a heterosexual identity —not always achieved without hurts, wounds, recriminations and retaliations not only from the parents but also from the partner. Adolescents and parents can become entangled in disturbing and unhappy life-long double-binds and Laingian-type knots unless the sensitive evolvements of mid-adolescence are achieved and the sometimes necessary re-enactments lead to de-escalation and reciprocal concern.

Here follow some problem areas in the parent-adolescent struggle in the face of sexuality and sex-partners. Where fixations of the past need to be broken, a battleground can ensue, e.g. insistence that all relationships should be baby-mother rather than adolescent-adult; that is, 'whole person ownership' is fought over. Then there is the 'part person ownership' battle, e.g. 'organ ownership' where the daughter, struggling with intrusive parents, needs to prove her vagina is her own and so runs off with a man. 'Ownership by another' is where the parents battle with the partner. Or there can be a battle to defend the parents' sacred emotional territory, i.e. the repressed areas in the family are now openly selected in outside pairing to break the symbiosis, or to contradict an incestuous link or to get revenge by exposing hypocrisy, for example, quiet, religious, law-observing, over-gentle father—with selection by the adolescent girl of a motor-cycling, irresponsible and rapistically aggressive skinhead. Actual territory or 'defensible space' can be fought for, for example, an adolescent girl who has to share a room with a younger brother gets privacy by indulging in 'secret' sexual encounters outside. Pairing and antipairing manoeuvres arise out of the politics of exclusion and one parent pairing with the adolescent against the other parent; or parents attack the emotional links of the adolescent with an outsider; or parents can only pair with each other *against* the adolescent.

101

Role reversal struggles and expressions, for example, strong mother, weak father, lead to the son selecting a homosexual partner because it is the father who is really the female parent.

The healthy parent can vicariously enjoy and share, be a helpful guide, appropriate and not too intrusive, over-restrictive or over-permissive. For example, parents who allow their fifteen-year-old daughter to stay out till two in the morning without knowing the truth of her whereabouts must somehow be colluding. Similarly, parents who treat her as a nine-year-old can expect repercussions. Non-restriction can be seen by the adolescent as non-caring. And this unhappy breaking of the parent-child bond can exaggerate acting-out to get the parents to care (i.e. to prolong the bond, even if hostile). Hostilities usually cover anxieties and uncertainties about sexuality in both parent and child.

In this so-called permissive age with drastic changes in authority structures and the relaxation of sexual mores, appropriateness of parent-child relationships is crucial. But what is 'appropriate' begs the whole question. In these times benign control must be combined with the delegation of some degree of emotional responsibility to the adolescent. 'Appropriateness' requires a mutual adjustment, empathy and understanding, not only of and by the parents but also of and by the adolescent.

Conflicts with parents there always have been. It is the partner who is now the prime focus even if there exists no parental cross-fire or complication. It is about now that the bio-sociopsychosexual territories begin to be more intimately and heterosexually explored. Progressions into new social, physical and sexual territories are made, interlinking with the emotional and psychological. The fantasies, the realities, the struggles, doubts, hopes, fears, advances, retreats involved in the struggles of making contact and finding a partner can be amongst the most poignant of human experiences. The fantasies, the 'crushes', the disillusionments, the eventual progressions to heterosexuality are profound experiences. Slowly, through the courage of advancing through, meeting, introducing, speaking, phoning, accompanying, dancing, touching, embracing, kissing, fondling and, as Freud says, 'fumbling', eventually, at some stage, the mechanics of sex are being made capable of being mastered. The emotions usually still need to be mastered as well as learning 'the language of love' and sex and discovering that love has 'a strange method of mathematics'. For instance, how or why or when there can or should be love minus sex, sex minus love, sex plus love. Or even, sadly, no sex and no love because no partner is felt ever likely to be found. And, eventually, beyond the mechanics and the mathematics.

Late Adolescence—convergence and consolidation

Hopefully, at late adolescence either the realistic aims of sexuality should have been achieved or there should be confident clues that these can be achieved. These states are usually characterised by a gradual evolvement of body, mind, emotions, technique and finding a partner, all of which converge into some more or less discovered and established feeling of sexual identity with the gestalt of *this is me* beginning to consolidate itself. The discovery of *who* one is, sexual identity-wise, can, if satisfactory, lead to joy. If not, to despair or to frantic attempts to achieve desired identity. Take the case of a seventeen-year-old boy whose sexual organs did not develop at puberty. He had a severely castrating mother. She would, for example, attack him bitterly for leaving on the electric lights in his bedroom when he went into the toilet or bathroom. For him to have refaced the Oedipal conflict to emerge through to adolescent sexuality would have put him unconsciously in mortal danger, for fear of castration by the mother, not the father, who had been emotionally castrated by her already. Eventually the boy ran away from home by climbing down a rope from his window late at night. Therapy had been commenced but broken off because his mother waited for him one day outside the clinic. (This is one instance where, were it possible, conjoint family therapy could have helped.)

Frequently, what on the surface may appear to be satisfactory heterosexual relationships can be founded on infantile modes, e.g. the partner in sexual intercourse is not a person but is used as a receptacle, or the sexual intercourse is not yet joined up with appropriate emotional feelings and is really a masturbatory act; or is a part-object relationship, e.g. the partner is selected because 'she has a nice pair of boobs'. Basically an emotionally satisfactory alternative to the Oedipal conflict has not been achieved and a pre-Oedipal stage and technique of relating is settled for, no matter how sophisticated it may appear on the surface.

At late adolescence the transition from the parents, emotionally at least, should be compensated by the establishment of a satisfactory heterosexual relationship, otherwise feelings of isolation, emptiness, despair or sophisticated defensiveness can become entrenched. Frequently, some heterosexual relationship is achieved but contains echoes of incompleteness which no amount of heterosexual intercourse or 'interchangeable props' can make whole. Often, rather than emotionally separate from the parents, the late adolescent can project the problem on to the parents and get them to keep interfering with his relationships. A girl of nineteen, a youngest child, continually skirmished with her parents over boys she dated. None was satisfactory in the parents' eyes. There appeared to be a collusion. The adolescent feared separating while the parents feared being left alone with each other, to face their own difficult relationship —to be husband and wife rather than parents.

Where *this is me* equals a confused, disrupted, fragmented identity, or the answer points to the possible consolidation of an identity not wanted or socially tabooed or otherwise disturbed, then despair can be great. Sometimes suicidal impulses can be powerful when the sexual identity is felt to be fractured or perverted. Unresolved residues, doubts, hopelessness, isolation, fragmentation, can overwhelm and nothing feels confirmed except disintegration and losing out.

The struggle with different degrees of bisexuality is one of the struggles of all adolescents and, indeed, of mankind, for the identities of both parents are introjected. Masturbation is an instance where the fantasy and action involves taking the role of both sexes. Adolescent patients who came to treatment several years ago because of bisexual impulses were deeply distressed. Today this is still so for many patients but less so for adolescents generally. Indeed, some adolescents can boast of their 'special superiority' because of their bisexual experiences or impulses. With Women's Lib, Gay Lib, Unisex and bisexual pop-star exhibitionism, societal attitudes to bisexuality and homosexuality seem generally less disturbing. However, to many adolescents this can be most distressing. So while sexual identity confusions and transitions are natural and normal during adolescent sexual development, the anxiety and persecution of these states (some more serious than others) can cause deep depression and fears of 'incurable' abnormality. On the whole, sexual identity confusion is one of the struggles of adolescence if not of life—e.g. menopausal man. It is contended by psychoanalytic writers like Winnicott that health is being in contact with the split-off feminine and masculine sides of oneself. Freud and the analysts claim that bisexual (not necessarily acted-out) impulses are never quite resolved throughout life. The poet exhorts us to

> *Leave doubt where doubt should be*
> *lest it be blinded by clarity.*

At the present time there are indications that adolescents are manifesting a more ambiguous sexual identity, not necessarily a bisexual one but a deeper degree of empathy with the feelings of both sexes, thus narrowing the once rigid polarisation of the sex differences. The whole concept of morality and dual morality is becoming less clear, e.g. adolescent girls can go boy-hunting and not wait, wall-flower like. These areas, together with the earlier onset of sexuality, seem to be in the forefront of adolescent sexual evolution (and revolution).

Despite overt 'cocksureness', adolescents can be very vulnerable in relationships. Loneliness, failures, rejections and unrequited loves, being used and dropped, can be very painful. Many adolescent suicides can have love and sexual unhappiness and identity confusion as a major cause.

Frequently sexuality can be used for entirely non-sexual purposes, e.g. as a defence against deep depression. But sexuality and sadness have links, for no love is love without knowing sadness and mourning (especially over the loss of profound and idealised love of the Oedipus complex).

Freud pointed out the healthy necessity of the joining of the sexual and the tender feelings. But there also needs to be a separation, a sorting out of the sexual and the aggressive feelings so that anger over past love-objects and relationships will not intrude so strongly as to disrupt healthy loving sexual relationships. Also necessary is the separation (but not entirely) of infantile needs from adult needs so that the giving up of self-gratifying needs can be replaced with the pleasure of empathy, mutuality and concern for one's partner. Without this no real wholeness in sexuality and identity is established. Isolation (non-pairing feeling) can result; or there can be schizoid feeling (even when pairing, the completeness cannot be experienced), or emptiness and loneliness, fragmentation, confusion; or no 'holding' relationships can result. There is no real 'refinding' of earlier idealised relationships and disillusionment can overshadow relationships. With this, there evolves, hopefully, not only body-mind-act alignment, but alignment between one person and another.

This is the rapprochement: the meeting of the two persons to experience deep reciprocal involvement that can surpass past fixations in ways that are loving, conciliatory and emotionally fulfilling rather than pain-inflicting and continuously littered with the debris of unforgotten emotional shrapnel.

But the achievement of wholeness of two persons, happily, healthily and sexually in love leads to one of the built-in paradoxes of maturity: two cannot be one, but linked must also allow each other a single separate wholeness.

It is reassuring for me that Freud[2] himself had the humility to confess in writing that he could not fathom all the enigmas constituting the essence of sexuality, while Winnicott offered this advice: 'My contribution is to ask for a paradox to be accepted and tolerated and respected, and for it not to be resolved. By flight to split-off intellectual functioning it is possible to resolve the paradox, but the price of this is the loss of the value of the paradox itself.' This quote is from his book appropriately entitled *Playing and Reality*.

REFERENCES

1. Peter Blos, *On Adolescence* (New York, Free Press, 3rd edn, 1967).
2. Sigmund Freud, *The Complete Psychological Works of Sigmund Freud* (London, Hogarth Press, 1968), Vol. 7, p. 243.

7

Sex Role Dilemmas of Modern Adolescents

ELISABETH HENDERSON

Introduction

There is a new wave of awareness about women's roles in society which has major implications for adolescents at the threshold of adult sexuality. The adolescent girl has to face not only her own personal turbulence at adolescence, but also a changing social situation involving her in uncertainty about the nature of personal and power relations between men and women. Changes in female roles affect male roles. This means the boy, too, is caught up in uncertainties about the nature of his identity.

Increasingly, sexual discrimination is being challenged. The general public understands better the attitudes and rationale behind the Woman's Movement, which is engaged in identifying and challenging sex-role definitions if these can be seen to underpin sexual discrimination. These efforts of the movement have led to a re-emphasis being placed on the social (as distinct from the biological or psychological) nature of sex-role identifications. This emphasis encourages us to take a fresh look at both the reasons for, and the nature of, the adolescent sex-role identifications of both boys and girls.

In this chapter I propose to take up some of the themes raised by the new academic literature about the psychology

108

of women and relate these to the problems of adolescence. Firstly I shall consider some of the premises used in this literature. Then I shall focus on how social factors affect development from adolescence to adulthood, looking not so much at psychological factors but more at those social notions of femininity, masculinity, and maturity which are internalised by adolescents. Lastly, I shall consider sex-role dilemmas which confront boys and girls at the adolescent stage.

The New Emphasis

The crisis of adolescence is often discussed primarily through the medium of the psychology of boys; a description of girls' development is grafted in as though their maturation is 'the same but different', along the line of a mirror image to that of boys. In fact the dilemmas of adolescent girls are by no means parallel. They are complementary. Analysis of the more neglected psychology of one sex means fresh light can be thrown on the psychology and development of both sexes. Such analysis confronts us with the way personal qualities have been divided between the sexes and how male norms are dependent on female ones which corroborate them and vice versa.

Popular and academic debate makes it possible to question models of parenthood and family without necessarily being seen as wishing to destroy their functions. Criticising the polarising nature of sex-role stereotypes need not be seen simply as a wish to attack the other sex, nor as an attempt to destroy out of hand social institutions with which we are familiar. It is hoped criticism may be seen as serious concern as to whether sex-role definitions need be so acute, over their human cost to both sexes, and whether the aims of, say, the family could be better served through different modes of co-operation between men and women. Since the turn of the century there have been enormous economic, political and social shifts in the status of women, and the momentum for change in these areas has not stopped. Today, however, the issue is not merely that of equalising with men, but also of evaluating the human consequences of such social concepts as 'men's work' and 'women's work', 'men's roles' and 'women's roles'.

In our own development we are all faced with the meaning of the difference between the sexes. How far do biological differences lead to social and emotional ones—to alternative roles and work for men and for women? The extent to which we believe in the separation of men's and women's work and roles depends on whether we believe the differences are biologically or socially determined, reflecting intrinsic human nature or social characteristics expected of male and female in our society. Most people, of course, would like to say the truth lies somewhere in between, but then they are faced with the question of just *where*.

Recently a number of writers[1,2] in the psychological field have begun to suggest that social conditioning plays a major part in the development of gender identity. Social cues and expectations, for instance, clearly influence the way a girl feels about herself as she asks, consciously or otherwise: who or what am I? What kind of person am I expected to be? She searches inside and outside herself for clues: do they lie in her own feelings and should her feelings coincide with the messages of the advert, the patterns of her parents, or her job opportunities. In this period of uncertainty it is easy to see how the adolescent will grasp the stereotype views which at least offer her the security of a consistent model of behaviour. People tend to have a strong sense of their gender identity derived from their consistent treatment as being of one sex or the other. It is easy to see how people accept sex roles, almost without question, as a way of placing themselves in relation to their fellow human beings. People accept this as a method of social placing because of the need for security knowing how to relate to others. Thus so many of life's tasks are allocated and made eligible on the basis of sex.

Knowledge about oneself in relation to the world is internalised by boys and girls so they do not need to ask in order to know how 'freaky' they would be if, at the extremes, girls wanted to be builders, furniture removers, or else boys to be nursery nurses, to learn cooking—although in other countries and other cultures these options by no means have the same bizarre connotation. Thus the definitions of sex roles which provide the basis of gender identity are internalised so that, when moving to new situations, girls and boys know what to expect of themselves and each other in terms of manners, attitudes, and economic opportunities.

Sex roles are not to be confused with sexuality. The relation between the two is very complex. Sexual impulses are normally channelled in ways that are socially acceptable and fit in with current sex-role definitions. Yet sexual expression may even conflict with prescribed sex roles at certain times and in certain cultures—as the stereotype Victorian Miss may have found to her cost. All the same, there is a developmental relation between the two as when children, poised at the edge of puberty, have to begin to explore adolescent sex roles in order to integrate their emerging sexuality and to find ways of relating to the opposite sex. It may be worthwhile looking at the way the formation of sex-role stereotypes is encouraged *prior* to adolescence in order to understand the divergence between boys and girls at that stage and to appreciate the different expectations and resources with which they meet adolescence.

The Effect of Sex-Role Stereotypes on Childhood Development

Howard Moss[2] suggests that right from birth girls and boys are handled differently by their mother according to her feelings and expectations about masculinity and femininity.

Much has already been said about the nature of Oedipal strivings and of the child's growth through identification. It is important to consider the actual *content* of these identifications, *what* the child is discovering about masculinity and femininity. For instance, to pick one factor in the boy's Oedipal struggle, the little boy reformulates his relationship with his mother by being *like* father. Yet the child's-eye-view of the big man or woman is likely to be based on an oversimplification or, we may say, a stereotype, which if left unmodified can leave the child brittle with inflexibility in personal relationships in later life. His attempt to identify with his father may involve a struggle to acquire what he sees as the characteristics of a *man*, separating out from his mother—not being 'a little baby' any more, 'a mother's boy', or 'a little sissy'—and in repudiating the dependency of infancy by standing up for himself, by being tougher, exploratory, and more independent. He picks up cues from his parents about 'maleness'. As Judith Bardwick and Elizabeth Douvan[3] say: 'When boys are pressured to give up their childish ways it is because these behaviours are perceived as feminine by parents.' Yet it is the mother who looks after him. There is a danger, as Jean Miller[4] points out, that a process is set in motion whereby the boy not only repudiates his identification with the mother, but also with the *processes* for which she is responsible, such as nourishing, feeding, active caring for needs and dependency. Where repudiation does happen the boy is likely to be impoverished in his development, particularly in relation to his own dependence and in coping with dependence and intimacy in others.

By contrast there is no such embargo on dependency in girls. Femininity is *not* defined as the opposite of babyhood but retains the major characteristics of babyhood: dependency, passivity, and receptiveness. The suggestion is that at the Oedipal phase girls do not have to earn their femininity because they will be seen as feminine if they remain dependent in their behaviour. Whereas the boy has to renounce babyhood and to struggle to gain a masculine identity, the little girl remains dependent and has *femininity* attributed to her.

The difference between boys and girls at this stage has been explained by saying that having or not having a penis leads to a different resolution of the Oedipus complex. But what is important is how the penis is valued. In our society where men earn, govern, and are given the opportunities to do so, it is easy to see that the penis is identified with male values and activities. It seems as though the thrust of the phallus symbolises the masculine principle of potency, achievement, logic and rationality. To identify with the man who has the penis means to identify with reason, with strength, and with prowess. What then does it mean to identify with the woman who does not have the penis when the penis is regarded as the symbol and the proof of these qualities?—Is it to identify with the opposite? Is it simply castration—*not* to be able to be creative, take the initiative, the logical, firm, and forthright? The problem may be that the child-bearing, reproductive work of women has been denigrated, undervalued in our male-valuing society, and is not sublimated by both sexes as care for the maintenance of life. This makes it difficult for the girl to have the feeling she can identify with the woman as a full human being in society.

Freud[5] saw the development of girls in *not* having. He thought that having a penis meant the boy has to cope with anxieties of being castrated, whereas the girl has to cope with the fact that she already has been. He felt that this led to greater superego development in the boy in terms of moral and ethical concern. Yet if the girl is encouraged to remain dependent on others, reliant on external authorities, judging herself to a great extent by the approval and pleasure of others, it is understandable if her inner controls and criteria for self-esteem are less than fully developed. The boy is encouraged to be less dependent on external authority and more on his inner representation of it, which readily leads to a more developed superego and to qualities of self-reliance.

Sex-Role Dilemmas at Adolescence

Thus we see how sex-role stereotypes (prior to adolescence) reinforce the differences between the sexes rather than shared areas of developing maturity and common characteristics. At adolescence one way of characterising the difference between the sexes may be in terms of a difference of emphasis between being *subject* or *object*. The subject acts directly upon the world in terms of individual will, choice, achievement, and self-serving. The object's relation to the

113

H

world is mediated by needing to fit in with the expectations and requirements of others. The object senses that in life it is others who prescribe the norms of what is appropriate behaviour and they who have to be pleased. It would not be true to make a clear-cut division with boys as subjects and girls as objects. The truth is much more subtle. The individual is sometimes subject and sometimes object. Working-class boys, for instance, are aware how much they are the object—a pair of hands, 'manual labour'—in the economic structure. Yet, by the late teens, in relations between the sexes the working-class boy may be the subject and the girl the object in the dynamics of their relationship. Both sexes have subjective experiences of their own lives. The difference may be that the girl's subjective experience is of being an object in *many* areas of her life. What we may see is that it is precisely when the girl is caught in conflict between being subject or object that she is precipitated into emotional conflict or a blunting of her personal growth.

Social messages and social options

The problem of the adolescent girl in working out her adult femininity involves conscious and unconscious questions about what sort of person she should be, which characteristics would make her desirable and successful, which goals are open to her and which closed. Part of the difficulty in assessing these questions may be that the social messages the girl receives are quite contradictory. At school she is caught up in an educational ideology which suggests that there are equal opportunities for men and women; that self-development should be sought by every individual, male or female; that there is encouragement for the girl to develop her skills and ambitions in a career. Yet, at the same time, this educational ideology is infiltrated by other attitudes which discriminate between the girl and boy. The boy is virtually barred from learning about parenthood when the subject on the curriculum is 'mother-care'! Similarly, cooking may be scheduled at the same time as engineering or woodwork so that pupils have to make an either/or choice which is underpinned by a direct bias to male/female distinction. The 'equal opportunity' educational ideology is thus infiltrated by a more traditional social ideology which puts pressure on girls not to develop past a certain point, to take service rather than management jobs and, in fact, not to invest too much in their careers. These attitudes cohere round a view of femininity which is the role-differentiated traditional one, incorporated in our economic system—that the woman rather than the man makes the family the priority in terms of work and time. In this view the woman is not essentially expected to achieve in her own light but to enhance and foster the achievement of her husband and children. Even when she works she is expected to fit best into supportive and service roles rather than productive ones, i.e. as a secretary, hairdresser, or nurse and, until recently, the woman's professions such as teaching, and social work.

The school situation shows the extent to which social institutions can mould adolescent development—for instance, by the simple message of the courses offered to them. One must also begin to wonder about the social message implicit in the school structure about male and female careers when, in mixed schools, the staff are so divided that men comprise the executive and women the broad base of the teaching hierarchy.

'The motive to avoid success'

The girl's identity must be affected by the career and self-development options posed as appropriate for her. Contradictory messages, however, are not just external to the girl, they are internalised by her, and form the basis of her personal dilemmas.

As Judith Bardwick and Elizabeth Douvan[3] puts it thus:

'While boys are often afraid of failing, girls are additionally afraid of succeeding. So the adolescent girl, her parents, her girl-friends and her boy-friends, see success as measured by objective, visible achievement, as antithetical to femininity. Some girls defer consciously, with tongue in cheek, but the majority . . . internalise the norms and come

115

to value themselves as they are desired by others. The only change from childhood is that the most important source of esteem is no longer the parents but the heterosexual partner.'

It is painful to imagine that a girl may experience so much confusion and anxiety over shaping a positive identity that she inhibits her own intellectual and personal interests. I am not in fact suggesting that a thirteen-year-old girl is aware of all the conflicts or even, necessarily, of the implications of her choices. Yet, as one traces the development of the average girl, one can see that at decisive points she chooses the arts rather than sciences, practical skills rather than intellectual development, work rather than further education. Mattina Horner[6] suggests that in girls there operates a 'motive to avoid success'. This is not the motive to be a failure, but the motive to avoid the kind of success that would price a girl out of the boy-friend market and preclude her from following her marriage and sexual aims. This conflict would only exceptionally (neurotically) be present in a boy: the more a boy achieves the more acceptable he is, the more he will be seen to provide and feel that he is a man worth having. Success does not diminish his masculinity; it enhances it. Popularity with the opposite sex and achievement are not set in conflict with each other for him. For an academic and career-minded girl they may well be.

Feminine desirability

The academic girl is aware that if she follows a career with the same zest as a boy who decides to be a professional, she may in fact have to make some kind of personal choice between career and feminine desirability. Too much emphasis on success at school-work may conflict with the more important aim of sexual attractiveness, making it counter-productive for a girl to define herself too clearly in the career area. The girl may be aware that the less she defines herself the more she can be defined by others and have, therefore, as wide a possible range of suitable boys to take her out.

116

The girl knows the boy may feel he just does not want to go out with a girl who will outrank him, who may even just show him up by comparison. If this is in any way hard to believe, imagine a girl who wants to go out with a boy who is shorter, slighter, younger and less bright, although having a very pleasant personality. This is a terrible description of a boy-friend but could easily match the requirements that a boy has of his girl-friend! It is in fact no easy thing for the boy to be the superior—it clearly involves an element of strain for him. Girls tend to choose the boy who is likely to be superior, older, in a higher class—colluding to maintain the imbalance.

The real question is whether career success means that a girl, of necessity, has to jeopardise her femininity, her relations with boys, and even to become masculine if she follows external ambitions. One might imagine that success and sexual attractiveness could merge together in a full human being. They do of course but only if the girl's friends, family, school, and job environment endorse the girl as feminine in pursuing objective achievement in the world. All too often, although the girl would like to combine femininity and ambition gracefully she is pressured to experience them as contradictory.

Many girls experience family pressures to do well at school and at college and yet at the same time not to do so, in order that they may still be seen to be feminine and get married. Here is a quote from Mirra Komarovsky's[7] study on cultural contradictions and sex roles. It is from a college student who writes:

'I get a letter from my mother at least three times a week. One week her letters will say: "Remember this is your last year at college. Subordinate everything to your studies. You must have a good record to secure a job." The next week her letters are full of wedding news... "When," my mother wonders, "will I make up my mind." Surely I wouldn't want to be the only unmarried one in my group. "It is high time," she feels, "that I give some thought to it".'

117

Female identification

The contemporary problems experienced by girls of the lack of opportunities for making personal and satisfying choices about work and marriage (or full-blooded combinations of the two) may be matched by earlier problems of finding satisfactory models of women with whom to identify. The traditional division of men at work, women at home— sociological phenomena—lead to profound psychological consequences, posing problems of identification for the boy and the girl. In developing her personal life-style, for instance, the adolescent girl needs to be able to identify with the woman as a *woman* if she is to feel happy to be one herself. The dilemma arises if the girl feels that the closest example at hand, her mother, is not a whole person, but only represents a half person, a home, non-intellectual, non-work-world person. If the girl has a leaning towards achievement in the work world or any desire for intellectual, academic, business, political, scientific achievement, then she may have to make a 'male' identification in these areas. This means that she is forced to identify with the characteristics which, traditionally at least, seem to belong to the opposite sex. She is likely to see and to label herself as a 'masculine' girl, repudiating her traditional sex-role, desexed, yet unable to find another version of femininity for herself, and therefore to see herself as merely competitive with men.

Unfortunately, as we have seen, there are many strands of thought in society which reinforce this view of the girl. Even psychoanalysis, which did so much for female sexual libera-tion, may have unwittingly contributed to these ideas. Very early in the development of analytic thought such terms as 'phallic woman' and 'penis envy' were coined. These may contain true insights about feminine problems. Yet there seems to be an inordinate time-lag for corresponding ideas of male envy of women's creativity to be accepted. There also seems to be a lack of corresponding labels for such concepts, such as for instance 'vaginal man' or 'breast envy'! These delays do seem to indicate a bias that a girl desiring skills regarded as masculine may in some way be thought to be aberrant.

In Freud's day the girl who wanted to achieve success in work areas which were then reserved for men only, having very little outlet for her ambitions, might easily become frustrated and envious. What has become clear is that sex-role stereotypes place restrictions on individual opportunities which easily lead to frustration or envy. The defensive manoeuvres with which girls cope with their ambitions are still with us. The competitive girl, feeling that ambition and femininity are in conflict yet wanting both, may become a castrating girl, tearing at her own and other people's in-adequacies. The 'feminine' girl may devalue herself but demand that the man she is attached to is super-powerful. Jettisoning her own ambition, she may try to satisfy it through her man who thus has to carry a double load of both his and her ambitions. The collusion where one sex has to express the ambitions and personal qualities of the other can be very cosy while it works, but when it breaks down, the fabric of the relationship is torn apart.

Problems of parental sex-role dilemmas

The breakdown of collusive sex-role choices may first impinge on the adolescent through parental sex-role dilemmas. If a mother has made the traditional choice of putting her husband and children as the primary focus of her activites, she may feel totally at a loss when there are no children left or they do not need looking after. Depression in middle-aged women is a well-known phenomenon. One factor may be that a woman reacts to the collapse of her role as a mother by depression and also with a sort of backlash possessiveness for her children who are likely to be just at the stage where they need space to test out their growing independence. Dan Greenberg[8] illustrates beautifully in his book *How to be a Jewish Mother* the way in which a mother can keep her son or daughter dependent on her throughout life by a judicious use of guilt, asking for attention from them in the present in return for her past caring, i.e. 'Look at

119

all I've done for you.' He points out, of course, that anyone can be, or have, a Jewish mother. The adolescent may succumb to the demands on him or her, or else be too close to do anything but react. For a girl the situation may be interpreted as a kind of immediate warning that the vocation of marriage and motherhood which is supposed to fulfill her, lived out her *mother's* way, can lead to depression and emptiness. Due to the emotional intensity of the relationship with the mother, an adolescent of either sex may want to break away and set up sexual relations which are primarily a reaction against the parents' marital set-up rather than based on a secure feeling of love, interest, or sexual attraction. For instance, the adolescent may be scared of developing deep or permanent relationships, preferring a pattern of rapid turnover relations in order to avoid the sort of desperate clinch of personal need which mother has demonstrated is intrinsic to her marriage. Also, in as much as the adolescent really cares for the mother, he or she is placed in a situation of extraordinary guilt in dealing with her. Leaving her is a kind of psychic murder, yet staying is psychic suicide. The loneliness and need of the mother in such a dilemma allows no middle way.

Sexuality

This fairly extreme example of the end result of sex-role differentiation, does nevertheless, highlight the way sex roles affect sexual patterns and even sexual feelings. Sexual feelings are not to be confused with sex roles, but, in practice, in sexual encounters the two do dovetail.

Many girls experience sexuality as hedged about with social anxieties and ambivalence—echoing their own inner feelings. The anxieties spiral around not only her unconscious fears of penetration, pregnancy, and sexual competition, but also around contradictory social expectations about femininity, sexuality, and promiscuity. However the girl defines 'sexuality'—she may see it variously as willingness to hold hands, to neck or else to have intercourse—if she is not 'sexual', she fears she may be called frigid, cold, or unattractive. If she *is* sexual, how sexual is she in fact to be? If she has sex, will she be popular or tarnished, attractive or just an 'easy lay'? The girl's anxieties are increased in that our culture makes quite clear to her that it is she, and not the boy, who is at risk. If she becomes pregnant, she, not the boy, suffers; if she takes contraceptives then she is admitting that she is the kind of girl who intends to have sex; if she will not have sex then she is a prude and has to suffer that label.

It is as though the culture plays on the girl's inner fears and offers her two alternative sexual identities. She may deal with her sexual anxieties by withdrawal into frigidity or else, if she rebels against inhibition, she may abandon her anxieties to become promiscuous. It is the old choice between the virgin and the whore.

These alternatives are reflected in the boy's attitude to girls. Most people accept that most boys will experiment with sex, if not actually go through a period of promiscuity. The girl with whom he experiments is an object—her significance lies in 'how far he can go' with her, in what he will be able to report to his peers. His feelings are likely to be reserved for the ideal and maybe untouchable girl. It is as though the adolescent boy approaches sexual encounters in the spirit of the Oedipal boy who has two attitudes to the same mother. One is of anger and denigration towards the sexual mother who goes off and leaves him; the second is of love for the beautiful, ideal mother who stays with him.

We can characterise the difference between the boy and the girl as being that the girl feels her choice lies in being either the virgin or the whore, whereas the boy reacts to each as he wishes. The question is: why is it the girl who is the object? Common terminology confirms that this is the case: the term 'sex object' refers to the girl. One person is only an object to another in a situation of dependency. To be an object is to allow others to determine one's value, one's good and bad points. A girl does this when she tries to become what her boy-friend wants, when she acquiesces to male views of feminine attractiveness and sexual desirability. The commercial world acknowledges this in the sphere of fashion

121

where female desire to please or dress competitively is big business.

It seems to me this dependency between boys and girls is grounded on the historical and continuing economic and social dependence of women on men. There is a pressure on a girl to marry, which is more than love and attraction, more than the desire to nurture a family: the motive of economic security backed by needs for emotional and social security affects her view of marriage. The girl is under pressure to learn to be a 'sexual object', to attract the male who will be able to protect and provide for her as she cannot for herself. A girl may then feel she must attempt to be chosen; passively or actively she takes the passive line. It may seem confusing that nowadays girls may take the initiative, may be loud rather than quiet in their manner, provocative rather than sexually modest. The question is whether the changes imply a change of attitude or a change of fashion in what is seen to be attractive, in what will draw the boy to the girl. The 'sexual liberation' may be more a change of fashion than a change in the basic mode of relations between boy and girl.

Sexual liberty does not necessarily lead to sexual pleasure or personal integration. In fact the loss of the protection of an arbitrary prudery may even make it difficult for a girl (or boy) to feel they have a rationale to withstand some sexual pressures or sexual advances.

Boys, girls, men and women love each other but even a relationship of 'dearness' is put under strain when the boy and girl approach sexuality and intimacy with such different experiences and expectations.

Conclusion

This has been a rather whirlwind journey through some of the issues raised by the new awareness of women's roles in society. We have looked at some of the ways sex roles militate against richer growth in development during adolescence. The idea of new modes of co-operation between men and women has been put forward. If new modes are evolved there may be some apparent loss of privilege for males. Yet we must consider the benefit to both sexes if the girl is freed of the constraints of being the object. If the girl is allowed a more highly valued view of her work, herself, her personal worth, given freedom to pursue her career and creativity, and to combine these with attractiveness and wishes to have a family, she will be able to give much more in her personal relations. The gain will be companionship and closer relations in the family and in co-operation at work.

Such developments imply tremendous changes in personal attitudes, and, more than that, imply a restructuring of our economic system so that it will be possible for men and women to work part-time, to involve themselves mutually in family activities, yet still to be seen as serious in their commitment at work and be available for promotion. We can imagine that men and women could share the housekeeping, could share the care of children, share the experience of personal development through a career. Such sharing would offer possibilities for people of both sexes to enrich their individuality and to develop the neglected facets of their own personalities. Such a vision would have seemed unthinkable in our society until very recently. Yet the recent economic upheaval in Britain, the three-day week implemented on the basis of a shift system, shows that such reorganisation is by no means impossible.

The beauty of adolescence lies in the adolescent freedom to be so many different kinds of people. The adolescent quicksilver experimentation highlights possibilities of human responsiveness and interaction. The rewards for all are clear if it is possible to safeguard the spontaneity and to minimise the world's pressures towards not the necessary, but the unnecessary structures of human interaction.

REFERENCES

1. Robert Stoller, *Sex and Gender* (London, Hogarth Press, 1969).
2. Howard A. Moss, 'Sex, Age and State as Determinants of Mother-Infant Interaction, *Marrill Palmer Quarterly*, Vol. 13, No. 1 (1967), pp. 19–36.

3. Judith M. Bardwick and Elizabeth Douvan, 'Ambivalence: The Socialisation of Women', *Readings on the Psychology of Women*, Judith Bardwick (ed.) (New York, Harper & Row, 1973), pp. 52–7.
4. Jean Miller, 'Psychoanalysis and Women', Jean Baker Miller, M.B. (ed.) (New York, Penguin Books Inc., 1973).
5. Sigmund Freud, 'Female Sexuality', *Psychoanalytic Quarterly*, Vol. 1, No. 1 (1931), pp. 191–209.
6. Matina Horner, 'The Motive to Avoid Success and Changing Aspirations of College Women', *Women on Campus:* 1970 Symposium, pp. 12–23.
7. Mirra Komarovsky. 'Cultural Contradictions and Sex Roles', *Readings on the Psychology of Women*, Judith Bardwick (ed.), (New York, Harper & Row, 1973), pp. 58–61.
8. Dan Greenburg, *How to Be a Jewish Mother* (London, Wolfe Publishing Ltd, 1966).

8

Adolescence and Politics: the Student Revolution

SUE HOLLAND

Anna Freud on 'young people', 1936:

'The philosophy of life which they construct—it may be their demand for revolution in the outside world—is really their response to the perception of the new instinctual demands of their own id, which threatens to revolutionise their whole lives.'

Students' wall slogan, France 1968:

'Be realistic, ask for the impossible.'

A concern with philosophical and political questions of a wide-ranging and world-shattering nature is *expected* of adolescents. Five decades ago a psychoanalyst, Anna Freud, could allay the anxieties of parents and teachers by explaining that the adolescent's preoccupation with such subjects as 'revolution versus submission to authority' was simply an aspect of the young person's struggle against the 'influx of libido'[1] characteristic of puberty. Parents could expect their pubescent children's political concerns to be as grow-outable as acne and spending too long in the bathroom.

The British students of the 1950s justified this expectation. They were mostly concerned with applying themselves to their studies and finding successful careers. They took light

125

relief in the form of rags and carnivals in which they might break a few things, including windows and their own necks. The authorities smiled on this benevolently as the antics of a favoured few who were having a last youthful fling before stepping soberly into adulthood. But the end of the fifties brought a huge increase in student numbers. The status quo was radically shifted. That decade closed with the Cuban Revolution, a revolution which was to symbolically inspire thousands of students of the next decade: a revolution led by young men against a corrupt and decadent regime.

Since the beginning of the sixties, for many adolescents the typical rebelliousness against authority has taken on a new collective and overtly political form. This is something more than the expected maturational confrontation with parental authority; the final renunciation of incestuous love objects; a differentiation from the family into independent adulthood. These adolescents are raising and contesting the basic political issues of who does what, who gets what, who is allowed to speak, and who decides. And the developmental period (if that is what it can be called) in which they do this is starting earlier and continuing later than any of the psychological theories on adolescence allowed for. Thirteen-year-old Londoners boycott classes to make a mass protest against arbitrary and undemocratic school authority, and thirty-year old American graduates stand trial on conspiracy charges for disrupting the workings of ballot-box politics. When windows are broken now it is not out of 'high spirits' but in the context of political protest and, as such, threatens the authorities who react punitively. For example, the disruption of a dinner party at Cambridge's Garden Hotel probably caused no more damage than romping students of earlier days, but because it was a political protest against the previous Greek regime the courts meted out harsh sentences (whilst at the same time denying that it was a political issue). In the American Kent University such legal niceties were bypassed and the military police sent in to quell campus protest with lethal effect.

What was thought of as a passing phase of adolescence is now becoming a more prolonged period of political protest

126

on such issues as racism and poverty, war and the military-industrial complex, and unrepresentative 'democracy'. So prolonged in fact, that psychology experts have suggested that this is not a phenomenon of 'adolescence' but an *optional* period of psychosocial development called 'youth'.[2]

A Breathing Space for 'Youth'

Post-adolescents who choose 'youth' before entering adulthood are presumed to be seeking an alternative channel of development. The underlying assumption is that such political protest will be abandoned on entering adulthood and the responsibilities of job, marriage, and family. Political protest is viewed as belonging only to a moratorium period of 'youth', and accommodation with the existing political system a necessary accompaniment of adulthood. So popular is this explanation that one psychoanalyst and student counsellor[3] recently told an audience who had come to be informed on the dynamics of 'student idealism and revolt' that Bertrand Russell, Marcuse, and Mao Tse-tung were, perhaps, 'perennial adolescents'. This is a convenient pseudo-scientific consolation for adults who have become so co-opted into the ruling social system they can no longer dare to take the risk of protest. The fact is that political passivity is not an automatic characteristic of adulthood but the risk of protest is less for adolescents unburdened by family ties and economic pressures.

A breathing space during adolescence allows for experimentation and exploration of personal potentialities, and at least opens the possibility that eventual compliance to society's expectations will be a matter of choice and not just a lack of imagination. The fact that so many young people today can choose a breathing space between school and work is one aspect of late capitalist societies which can afford to give some of its members time-out from producing and maintaining the economic system. Indeed, it demands a pool of unemployed labour, and the term 'youth' may be just a more euphemistic way of describing so many unemployed young adults. The tremendous growth of 'youth centres', particularly for young Blacks, is one aspect of this.

The apparent paradox is that of those young people who have chosen to fill in that 'breathing space' with a commitment to political protest, very many are the privileged and educated children of the white middle classes; children who would have everything to gain, materially, by complying with a social system which favours and rewards them. But these same pampered children are proving difficult to co-opt with offers of material gain. The psychoanalyst Maud Mannoni,[4] speaking of the French student revolt of 1968, points out that: 'A generation faced with a world based on having, rose to defend its right to exist in terms of being.' Mannoni ignores the fact that the larger world the students faced was as much based on not having as on having. But it is true that these privileged students seemed more concerned with such things as 'self-realisation' and the quality of human existence than the mere satisfaction of material needs. (It was an ironic lesson for the students when the Communist Party-led workers capitulated to the State for a wage increase.)

This concern with expression showed itself clearly in the Nanterre psychology students' boycott of their lectures. Their wall writings proclaimed that their total rejection of modern Western psychology was a 'reaffirmation of personal liberty, of the innocence of desire, of the forgotten joys of creativity, play, irony, and happiness. . . .' If such manifestos are really a response to the upsurge of instinctual demands characteristic of adolescence which Anna Freud spoke of, then it seems that these demands are accepted and met with great delight. The newly emergent clamours of the 'id' are not a threat to be defended against, but a supporting voice in the demand for a new non-repressive society. The typical pre-adolescent 'latency' period is a conforming, desexualised, over-intellectualised phase which is acceptable to society's authority-holders because it mirrors the prevailing norms of society. Because adolescence is an emergence *out* of this phase, it is also a phase of greatest conflict with those authorities.

More fundamentally, students all over the Western world

are now asking themselves and their teachers: 'Whose interests do these diciplines serve?' Many students, and now even schoolchildren, are demanding *knowledge,* not simply 'an education' to fit them neatly into the employment slots allotted for them. Those students who have chosen social science and humanities as their subjects of study tend to be the most vociferous in this demand. It is not only that the more questioning student is already predisposed towards an interest in these subjects, but that the very nature of human sciences stimulates the development of a reflexive critique. Because they offer an analysis of the nature of societies and of Man, they can be turned back on themselves to make the student's own society, and his own nature, the object of study. However much these sciences may be bourgeois, ideological buttresses for shoring up the status quo,[5] the examination of how things *are* can provoke a radical exploration of how things *could be.* This is the 'logical' internal dynamic of human science education which, Marcuse claims, inevitably leads to politicisation of students within the university.[6]

Authority-Conflict and Value-Conflict: Exposing the Contradictions

The most characteristic feature of student political protest of the sixties whether American, British, French or German, was its anti-authoritarian stance. In this sense it was enthusiastically anti-capitalist, as exemplified in the May 1968 slogan: 'The boss needs you, you don't need him.' But also anti-communist, at least in its dislike of Stalinist forms of bureaucracy and instinctual repressiveness.

During its early days the new politics of the student radicals rejected most of the tenets of orthodox left-wing theory, such as the need for mass working-class organisations and the building of a revolutionary party which could wrest power from the capitalist state. They preferred to identify themselves as a new revolutionary class, the modern oppressed of affluent capitalism, and experimented with forms of 'direct democracy' within their educational establishments.

I

Any emergence of structure was discouraged. Leadership was often denied, and the making of 'student leaders' such as Cohn-Bendit, Rudi Dutschke, and Tariq Ali, explained as a product of the establishment's attempt to isolate 'red agitators' within an otherwise uncomplaining mass of hard-studying, grade-orientated students. A programme, or even the most blurred of blueprints for a future mode of society was anathema to most of them, preferring to argue that an exploration of means would determine the ends.

The tactics of choice were those involving spontaneity and forms of direct action. Sit-ins, walk-outs, boycotts, publication of secret official documents, street demonstrations, and a variety of disruptive and norm-violating techniques were employed which drove the authorities to react with embarrassment, placatory negotiations, capitulations, police action, and even military suppression.

Central to all of these tactics is the aim of exposing the conflict of values inherent within modern Western society; the discrepancy between held liberal, humanistic ideals and the practice of such ideals; the credibility gap between the hopes and promises of Western democracy and its actual performance. Young people have always been peculiarly adept at laying bare the conflicts in their elders, but, as one study of 'campus disorders' suggests, this collectively organised exposure of value conflicts is a recent phenomenon.[7] Many of this generation of students are less willing than their predecessors to accept conflict-avoiding explanations. They have developed an arsenal of techniques for exposing the basic conflict of values in the system, including 'provoking', 'unmasking', and 'countercoercing'. It has not escaped psychologically sophisticated students that institutions with inbuilt contradictions may be analogous to neurotic individuals in that they require defensive and irrational behaviours to maintain these contradictions. In addition, there seems to be developing among modern 'youth' a life-style which is in itself conclusive to this type of confrontation; a life-style of 'explicit congruity'[2] in which young people strive to act overtly as they think and feel. The recent flood of literature describing the tactics and philoso-

130

phy of student activists tends to suggest that this is so: one thing these students are not, in their political protest, is Machiavellian.

Psychoanalysis on Action and Political Protest

It is this inclination to *act* upon thought and feeling, to make beliefs a public fact, that has led some psychoanalysts to explain student political involvement as an 'acting-out' of intrapsychic conflicts. Political action is then reduced or explained away as a displacement of an internal crisis. As, for example, in Shield's statement that: 'the radical student is inclined to fasten on to or create an external crisis in order to distract himself from his own internal crisis'.[3] Such an explanation fails to differentiate between action and 'acting-out'. Psychoanalysts of the Lacanian school[4] have corrected this failing by pointing to the fundamental difference between the two. Whereas 'acting-out' is characterised by an impulsive performance staged in the outer world but arising from an inability to regulate an inner conflict, action functions to reveal and actualise what was hidden or what one could not or did not want to see or know. It conveys a reality which can only be revealed by this means. For example, when students demonstrate on the streets to a point at which the military is called out to suppress them, this reveals for all to see that authority is force.

Because psychoanalysis explores not only what humans are but what they can hope to be, it can support (or undermine) the prevailing doctrines of a society. Psychoanalytic explanations of radical political protest have tended to shore-up the status quo by explaining such dissent in terms of individual pathology, while at the same time psychoanalysts claim scientific 'neutrality'. Psychoanalytic reduction of political protest to pathological 'acting-out' betrays an inherent difficulty within psychoanalysis itself which has not yet been solved; that is, the problem of action. Psychoanalytic therapy aims to liberate energy, or 'libido' which has been deployed in maintaining neurosis, but it expects the 'liberated' client to accept an unliberating society. Norman

O. Brown criticises that it 'fails to direct the libido back to the external world in the form of a project to change the world; by the same token it fails to provide a solution to the problem of aggression'.[8] It is not surprising, then, that orthodox analysts see in almost every actively protesting radical a 'problem with aggression', a 'problem with authority'. Apart from the fact that it is a tautology to *explain* the actions of those who struggle to change the structure of political authority as a 'problem with authority', it could also be the case of the analytic profession's 'projection' of its own internal problem on to its client, i.e. the problem of action.

But if pure psychoanalytic explanations of 'the student revolt' have been reductive and conservative, sociological-cum-psychological-cum-psychoanalytic ones have been hardly more enlightening. Take, for example, the 'political socialisation' literature.

'Political Socialisation'

In spite of its enormous increase, the 'political socialisation' literature concerned with the childhood beginnings of political behaviour has not offered much explanation as to the childhood antecedents of 'deviant' forms of political behaviour such as extra-parliamentary protest. This probably stems from the fact that this literature adopts the usual functional organic model of society in which socialisation is viewed simply as the presentation of what it is allowed to the person to become and of how he learns to become it. There are two main stages to this process: the first, in which the child 'identifies' with the parents (primary socialisation) and the second, in which the child learns to 'internalise the culture of society' and the appropriate roles (secondary socialisation).[9] The trouble with this approach is that it does not account for deviation or a notion of 'self' which is not just the sum total of roles learned. Nor does it highlight the possibility that the family and society may transmit non-complementary roles. Likewise, the 'political socialisation' literature reflects the same faults as the socialisation literature in general, in that it is unable to sufficiently account for changes both in individuals and in political systems.

But what this literature does show is that it is during childhood that some of the basic attitudes about political systems begin to take shape. For example, Easton and Dennis[10] propose that the attitudes towards political authority that are learned early will have some impact on the operation and future stability or change of that particular system in which socialisation occurs. One of the most important of these attitudes for the stability of a political system is 'a sense of the legitimacy of the authorities'; an acceptance that the authority roles such as government, have a right to hold power over others.

Certainly this generation of adolescents seems somewhat deficient in this 'sense of the legitimacy of the authorities'. But how early is this learned? There is mounting evidence that at least the roots of it are learned in that political microcosm, the family.

The Family and 'Authority Transference'

One frequent explanation for the modern student's apparent indifference to the legitimacy of institutional authority is that it stems, developmentally, from the 'abdication of the father' in the modern Western family.[11] Central to this view is the notion of 'authority transference' as a dynamic of political behaviour. This assumes that because the family, like the wider political system, has some members who hold authority over others, the formative roots of later attitudes to political authority will be found in early attitudes to parental authority.

Underlying this 'authority transference' hypothesis are the psychoanalytic concepts of 'identification' and 'introjection' through which the child incorporates characteristics of the parent because of Oedipal conflicts and feelings of vulnerability and helplessness. As the original feelings of aggression and fear towards the powerful parent then give way to positive affection, the child's first images of other powerful authority figures such as presidents or policemen will be

133

equally as admired. Hess and Torney[12] in their studies of 'childhood politicisation' state: 'The child who perceives his father as strong tends to be more attached to figures and institutions in the political system, particularly president and policeman, than the child who perceives his father as relatively weak.' The assumption here is that the family authority structure reflects the existing social order. Deference to a powerful father 'transfers' to become deference to political 'father figures'. A critic of the family, Wilhelm Reich,[13] pointed out that it was through just such a dynamic that the family produced new members whose psychic structure corresponds to the existing social order. Such individuals would not challenge that order through political revolt. The family had the political function of serving as 'a factory for authoritarian ideologies and conservative structures'. Reich was too pessimistic about the family to see its anti-authoritarian possibilities. He did not predict the student revolt of the sixties and the contribution of family politics to this.

The researches on families of student radicals indicate that the model of the feared and powerful father is not very frequent; partly because many modern fathers are less inclined to be role models for presidents and policemen, and partly because many modern mothers, being educated and wage-earners themselves, challenge the traditional model of paternal authority. These families tend to be non-authoritarian; there are reciprocal rights between family members, father has little formal authority as a 'boss', there is identification with *both* parents, and an emphasis on self-regulation, expressivity, and the attainment of 'ideals' rather than achievement of occupational status. These are interpersonal patterns and social values which hardly correspond with the educational, occupational, and governmental institutions of this society.

The parents in these 'protest prompting' families are socialising their children according to what they believe are the explicit values of a democratic society; for example, as embodied in the American Constitution, but these values are not congruent with other more implicit values dominant in

134

the institutional sphere. Such families are not serving a function of socialising individuals to fit into the society; on the contrary, as long as the institutions remain unchanged, they are socialising them *not* to fit in. In these cases, family ideology is in conflict with institutional ideology. Radical political protest may be one consequence of such a contradiction.

Internal and External Worlds: the Conflict

Two broadly disparate views are represented by the literature on the family and individual dynamics of young political activists. The one contingent, represented for example by Shields[3] and Lesse,[11] proposes that the present-day upsurge of student political protest arises from hostile conflict with, or 'abdication' of father, rebellion against parental values, poor ego development and emotional immaturity. The other, represented by such as Kenniston[14] and Flacks,[15] proposes that it springs from reciprocity in parent-child relationships, 'living-out' of parental values, strong ego development, and emotional and moral maturity.

In terms of empirical research, the evidence tends to favour the latter contingent. However, although there may be relative degrees of 'pathology' underlying the political views and behaviour of any young activist, it is contradictory for the defenders of student radicals to exaggerate the 'healthy' qualities of their subjects. To describe radical activists purely in terms of 'health' ignores the dialectic, that is the continual interpenetration between individual and society and the continuous circle of causes and consequences which result. An individual who is protesting that the society and its institutions are 'sick' cannot have escaped totally from the effects of these institutions such as family, school, and workplace. Student politicos are not immune to neurotic unhappiness in a society in which psychological illness is almost as prevalent as the common cold.

Recent psychoanalytic theory proposes that the main driving force in human behaviour is not the desire for instinctual gratification, but for meaningful relations with other people; 'object seeking' rather than 'satisfaction-seeking'[16] The

135

activist's political philosophy such as 'direct democracy', 'socialism', etc., expresses an implicit hoped-for relationship with others but it is one projected into the future. Here, the existentialist notion of human 'project' or 'life-trajectory' can convey a psychosocial phenomenon which is overlooked or explained away by other psychologies. When humans are viewed as projecting themselves into the future, the notion of identity must be similarly broadened to include these strivings in relation to others. Kenniston holds that today's young radicals have linked their own newly emerging identities with an emerging movement for social change. Because of this 'fusion of inner identity with ongoing historical process', it may be that the radical achieves identity 'only with the sociopolitical transformation he seeks'.[14] If Kenniston is correct, the young political radical does have an 'identity problem', but a special one.

The German psychoanalyst, Mitscherlich, suggests that overt or covert protest is characteristic of adolescence but that the present political rebellion of youth is not reducible to just maturational crisis. He proposes that there are 'experiences of unpleasure and discomfort which are not resolvable by habituation and adaptation' which are at the core of the self-awareness and political views of these rebels.[17]

Perhaps *one* of these 'experiences of unpleasure and discomfort' is the discrepancy between an expressive, democratic family life and a restrictive hierarchical institutional life. The problem for students from such families will be how to fit what has been learned and 'internalised' in the family into the institutional setting: active attempts to alter the institutions may be one solution.

Here, the 'authority transference' hypothesis would be more useful if it abandoned the orthodox analytical view that only the 'objects' (family authority figures) which are in some form taken into the personality of the individual make him react towards other 'objects' (political authority figures) in a manner which resembles that individual's reaction to the, now internalised, family figures. It is more relevant to an understanding of political behaviour to regard family *systems* or *modes of interacting* as the phenomena which are internalised in childhood, and systems or modes of interacting as the political phenomena which are reacted to in later life. The notion of internalisation of family interactions as outlined by Laing in his account of *The Politics of the Family* is useful here;[18] although Laing tends to take the 'defence mechanism' view of the process and sees the child as caught in an unending series of interlocking 'projections' and 'introjections' from family to society and vice versa. He ignores the more optimistic possibility that the family, under certain conditions, can provide the personal resources which enable the child to recognise and question some of those 'rules' which, Laing claims, are not even acknowledged as rules in this typically mystifying society.

If the 'authority transference' hypothesis has any explanatory value in the case of the majority of student activists, it is that these young people expect institutional authority to be as benign and democratic as family authority and then react with critical protest on discovering this is not so. Schaffner implied something of this kind in his study of the families of Nazis and anti-Nazis, saying: 'The group opposed to authoritarianism when adults as a result of rebellion against authoritarian parents is smaller than those who oppose authoritarianism as adults because they were taught to in the home.'[19] It is not so much that certain values are learned or that certain persons are identified with—though this is important—but that whole patterns of interaction— how people behave towards one another—are internalised. These patterns may then later affect the way the person interprets and attempts to act upon society.

The paradox is that, though orthodox analysts lament the 'abdication of the father' because they believe it is the prime cause of 'the student revolt', psychoanalytic theory radically challenges the power of the autocratic father and the punitive superego. It is psychological and psychoanalytic notions about child-rearing that encourage self-expression and democracy within the family, and which have probably contributed to the wave of rebellion on the university campus of the sixties. It was the 'Spock-marked' babies who would later stand on the anti-war picket lines (along with Dr Spock himself). As another paediatrician, Winnicott, expressed it: 'that rebellion belongs to the freedom that you have given your child in bringing him or her up in such a way that he exists in his own right. In some cases it could be said, "You sow'd a baby, and you reaped a bomb".'[20]

Disappointments and New Beginnings

When adolescents put themselves into 'a project to change the world', they take on no easy task. The external world is hugely complex and each series of actions to change it leads to numerous counteractions and unforeseen consequences.

During the last few years, students have experienced an increasing sense of lost hopes, disappointment, and disillusionment with their previous political efforts. In the way of 'consultation', 'representation', and course-structuring they have achieved modest reforms without really changing the power structure within the universities. Outside that microcosm, the Vietnam War dragged on and then shifted to Cambodia, the megalopolises increase their profits and their redundancies, and unemployment, poverty, and racism shows no sign of abating. This sense of impotence in the face of a too powerful opponent is pungently expressed by Jerry Rubin of the Youth International Party (Yippies) in his 1969 'emergency letter to my brothers and sisters in the movement' in which he conveys the despair and fear which has followed in the wake of the retaliations meted out by the American state on its young protesters: 'If America's own children—the brats of her white middle class—insist on acting like blacks, well, shit they will jail and kill us too.'[21] Despondency and political withdrawal has been the reaction of many adolescents, but another reaction has been an increasing and overtly violent militancy. The hard-core, cell-disciplined, bomb-throwing 'Weathermen' in the USA, the 'Red Army' in West Germany and the 'Angry Brigade' in Britain are one manifestation of where those once non-violently protesting but now grown elderly 'youth' are going.

On the British campus there have been signs that the

nature of student political protest is changing. The 1970 Labour Party's bestowal of the vote at eighteen seemed to be ignored by many students who continued to prefer extra-parliamentary politics or a withdrawal from politics altogether. A Tory government came into power. There is now less flamboyant disruption and confrontation within the universities over issues of internal government. Issues now tend to be around political victimisation of staff and students, the domination of big-business interests, the rising cost of student facilities, and state interference in student unions. The student unions themselves, once governed by right-wingers, liberals and pacifists, are now led by Communist Party members and they in turn are seen as too orthodox and reformist by sections of the student population.

Because much larger numbers of young people now enter further education, the sense of special privilege which earlier students accepted has been reduced. In fact, hidden subsidies which past students enjoyed have actually been curtailed with the increasing emphasis on cost efficiency and productivity which accompanied the expansion. Universities are no longer expected to produce a small elite of liberally educated, 'rounded' people but large numbers of specifically skilled scientists, educators, technicians and social-engineers. Degrees are no longer the rare and position-guaranteeing tickets they once were, and management's suspicion of the products of recently politicised universities has reduced the chances for even those decreasing numbers of graduates who still want to enter industrial management. As the Chairman of the Confederation of British Industry pointed out in a recent television appearance, modern university graduates seem to question the very principle of profit-making on which industry is based, and for this reason many industrial firms now prefer to train their own people.

As modern universities gear themselves to producing, not an elite, but an ever-increasing labour force, the students themselves are increasingly 'dropping out' and attempting to form their own counter-cultures, or are turning towards an identification with the working classes and examining their

139

own position within them. There is a trend towards forging links with the Labour movement, with apprentices in polytechnics, with grass-roots community organisations, and with schoolchildren. Last year some students combined with their catering staff in a collective protest against redundancies and increased costs of food; this year students all over the country are linking their fight against low grants and increased costs with Labour movement struggles against the wage freeze, rising prices, and increased rents. Many students not only join strike picket lines but contribute lump sums of money out of student-union funds. This is a very different population of students from that of the days of the 1926 General Strike when so many of them acted as volunteers to break strikes.

It is not the biological-instinctual process of adolescence which has changed, but the social experience of being an adolescent. Only in this historical era have adolescents developed a collective identity; cultural, economic and political.

Not Just Psychic Process but Historical Process

The type of person which universities expect to produce is not only in direct contradiction with the type of personality and expectations produced and encouraged by many of the families of students, but is the complete opposite of what was encouraged and developed in nursery schools with their emphasis on expression, imagination, and co-operative work-play. So the individual is not only in conflict with the university and career system but the educational system is itself in a state of contradictory conflict. Just as the families described earlier are socialising their children *not* to fit the social system, nursery and junior schools are doing the same. Adolescents find themselves not only having to cope with the turmoil of newly emergent sexual feelings and hormonal changes, but also the cognitive dissonance and inner-outer conflict which these inbuilt contradictions in the social system are almost bound to create. Active attempts to alter such a system is one way the adolescent may use to deal with the problem. It is the basis of political action, and by choosing this method rather than other solutions such as adaptation or withdrawal, adolescents begin their politicisation.

When adolescents are viewed in their social system the 'explanation' of their political protest becomes much more complex than the notion of an inner conflict which is *avoided* by turning to the external world. Such a simplistic notion ignores the dialectical relationship between the individual's inner psychic structure and the outer social system. Inner conflicts which have their counterpart in the external world may be, not avoided, but *confronted* and solved through action to change the external world. By such actions both the external world and the inner self are changed.

To argue that inner conflicts can only be solved intra-psychically is to employ a theory which is only half a theory; only half of the dialectic between inner and outer worlds. The beliefs and actions of adolescents must be seen within a social, historical process in which it is becoming apparent that many of today's adolescents are growing up to see external reality, to interpret it, and to try to change it. Their 'demand for revolution in the outside world' is not reducible to 'really' a response to their newly emergent and revolutionising instinctual demands. But rather, these psychic energies of adolescence can be powerful allies in the struggle for a social revolution from which many of their elders have opted out.

REFERENCES

1. Anna Freud, *The Ego and the Mechanisms of Defence* (London, Hogarth Press and the Institute of Psycho-Analysis, 6th impression, 1966), p. 177.
2. Paul Miller, 'Social Activists and Social Change:' The Chicago Demonstrators', *American Journal of Psychiatry*, Vol. 126, No. 12 (June 1970), pp. 94–101.
3. Robert Shields, lecture delivered at British Psychoanalytic Society, Winter lectures 1970, mimeographed copy.
4. Maud Mannoni, 'Psychoanalysis and the May Revolution', *Reflections on the Revolution in France: 1968*, Charles Posner (ed.) (Harmondsworth, Penguin Books, 1970), pp. 215–24.

5. Trevor Pateman (ed.), *Counter Culture* (Harmondsworth, Penguin Books, 1972).
6. Herbert Marcuse, *An Essay On Liberation* (London, Allen Lane, The Penguin Press, 2nd edn, 1969), pp. 61.
7. John Spiegel, *The Group Psychology of Campus Disorders—A Transactional Approach* (mimeographed copy from Lemberg Center for the Study of Violence, Brandeis University, Waltham, Massachusetts).
8. Norman O. Brown, *Life Against Death* (London, Sphere Books, 2nd impression, 1960), p. 138.
9. Talcott Parsons, 'General Theory in Sociology', *Sociology Today*, Merton, Broom and Cottrell (eds) (New York, Basic Books, 1959).
10. D. Easton and J. Dennis, *Children in the Political System* (Maidenhead, McGraw-Hill, 1969).
11. Stanley Lesse, 'Revolution, Vintage, 1968—A Psychosocial View', *American Journal of Psychotherapy*, Vol. 4, pp. 584–98.
12. R. Hess and J. Torney, *The Development of Political Attitudes in Children* (Chicago, Aldine, 1st edn, 1967).
13. Wilhelm Reich, *The Mass Psychology of Fascism* (New York, Orgone Press, 1946).
14. K. Kenniston, *The Young Radicals* (New York, Harcourt, Brace & World, 1968).
15. R. Flacks, 'The Liberated Generation: An Exploration of the Roots of Student Protest', *Journal of Social Issues*, Vol. 23, No. 3 (1967), pp. 52–75.
16. W. Fairbairn, *Psycho-Analytic Studies of the Personality* (London, Tavistock, 1952).
17. Alexander Mitscherlich, 'Introduction to Panel on Protest and Revolution', *International Journal of Psychoanalysis*, Vol. 50 (1969), pp. 103–8.
18. Ronald Laing, *The Politics of the Family* (London, Tavistock, 1971).
19. Bertram Schaffner, *Father Land: A Study of Authoritarianism in the German Family* (New York, Columbia University Press, 1948).
20. Donald Winnicott, 'Adolescent Processes and the Need for Personal Confrontation', *Playing and Reality* (London, Tavistock, 1971), p. 145.
21. Jerry Rubin, 'An Emergency Letter to My Brothers and Sisters in the Movement', *Bamn*, Stansill and Mairowitz (eds) (Harmondsworth, Penguin Books, 1971), p. 244.

9

Adolescence and Creativity

JUDITH ISSROFF

The notion that adolescence and creativity are linked in some special way is widespread; it is implied by a title such as the present one, and the two topics are discussed together in a rapidly growing body of literature.[1] But is this link a genuine one? Or is it perhaps a development of our increasing pre-occupations with the manifestation of adolescence and our simultaneous concern with the springs of creativity? I think it is probable that there are no particular associations between adolescence and creativity, whether the latter word is used in a wide sense to refer to that general activity by which men of any age group endow and vitalise their world,[2] or in the narrower sense to mean the productiveness of specially gifted individuals.

On Creativity

Each individual is born with his own possible creative ability. The degree to which this ability is eventually expressed is dependent on the developmental level that he will attain. That level is determined by the extent to which environment actualises ability. No matter how suitable the environment may be, if the genetic endowment is small, the capacity for creative expression and productivity will be

143

limited. On the other hand, no matter how richly gifted an individual may be in his innate creative ability, if his environment fails to meet his needs, he may never develop, experience or express his creative talents.

An individual's peak creative ability may be expressed at any age; some reach a peak early as child prodigies, and then peter out, others express it constantly throughout life, while still others are most prolific at an old age. To what extent this is genetic and to what extent environmental we do not know.

Thus there is a whole range of creative expression, a continuum from, at the one end, that of an infant playing with sound, and at the other, the 'genius'.

Man's distinguishing feature is his capacity for manipulating symbols.[3] Because of this he is not dependent solely on his genetic make-up or on his immediate environment, for he is able to communicate his experience; he can record and store it in such a way that the actions and imaginings of past generations become accessible in the present. This body of accessible information, which becomes available to each successive generation as it grows up, I shall refer to as our common non-genetic heritage, the collective mind of mankind (or, in simpler terms, human knowledge).[4]

Of course different individuals will contribute to or draw from this body of human knowledge in varying degrees. It is true that when we think of significant contributors, certain names spring to mind: Newton, Leonardo, Einstein, Goethe, Mozart; but we should not forget that creativity is as natural as breathing.[5] The creativity which maintains the structure of everyday life is the nutrient for that creative activity which is expressed by the specially gifted; without it, they could not function. It is obvious, to anyone who cares about the arts, that 'the good spectator also creates' (Swiss proverb). Creativity lives as much in the moment of appreciation as in that of conception.

I would like to restate these points for emphasis:

Nothing can come of nothing. My creative output stimulates yours. If other men do not appreciate or use particular products or ideas, the greatest human achievements would be ephemeral. They could no more exist beyond the moment than the individually significant (because personally integrative) symbolic creativity of, say, a dream, of children playing, of an adolescent day-dreaming, or of a schizophrenic neologising. For most people this normal, necessary symbolic creativity is sufficient to maintain personal integration. It does not necessarily result in a created end-product. At any age, the expression of creativity may serve a special function in maintaining personality structure (the ego organisation that a person employs to deal with his world, his personal private world as well as outer shared reality). There are others who may need to be specially inventive and productive in the use of their individual creative talents and abilities in order to integrate and feel integrated, who define themselves and need to be identified by their particular special functioning and production. In so doing they may make significant contributions to the sum of human knowledge.[3]

Because there are no short cuts to knowledge, the period of adolescence is of necessity increasing, both in duration and in the significance of the psycho-social moratorium[6] that precedes adulthood. The term 'adolescent' can no longer refer only to those aspects of development relating to the physical changes of puberty.

Whilst I believe we must cherish and encourage the specially gifted, we must not forget that creativity is absorbed in the flux of ordinary human daily activity (e.g. language, wit, decoration, play, dreaming, cooking, problem-solving and so on).

So, creativity is a universal human activity which belongs not only to those who blend sounds to disturb and delight us, not only to those who play with their visions, words or other symbols, with shapes, elements, textures or light, or with science and technology, marketing or newsprint but equally to those who are appreciatively involved with life, and the products of others, who are inventive and imaginative in the realm of human relations.

I defined creativity as *that with which we endow and vitalise our world*. As such, it is creative ability expressed in

145

a baby's way that is the basis for that baby's capacity to engage with and begin to relate to the world.

In the infant's inner life, relationships are based on his capacity to create, which at this stage means to find something resonant with his inner world and needs.[7] Later feelings of the reality of self and the world, of creative apperception, self-confidence and the capacity sympathetically to meet the needs of others is dependent on a meeting between, on the one hand, the infant's creative capacities and, on the other, assimilable portions of reality—Winnicott's 'doses'—with which the infant can deal meaningfully, and which the infant can thus come to feel it has 'created'. It is the internalisation of the reflections of other people which enables each of us to build our selves. This is a lifelong task which requires its own kind of creative ability. As Winnicott puts it, 'It is the creative apperception more than anything else that makes the individual feel that life is worth living.... Our theory includes the belief that living creatively is a healthy state.'[8]

What of someone whose creativity has been stultified? Feelings of alienation, complaints of feeling 'cut off' or bored and uninvolved, of unreality of self or the world, as well as feelings of deadness, are to some extent manifestations of a dissociation in the personality or a repression of the ability to live creatively. This probably stems originally from environmental maladaptation or insensitivity to the infant's creative capacities. But such environmental insensitivity may continue at later stages, indeed throughout life, and will always reduce an individual's capacity to make use of the world's cultural riches as well as his own talents.

Before I consider the questions of how we can evaluate the creative products of adolescence and promote the creative potential of our young, I would like to make some general remarks about adolescence and then briefly to comment on current society, not only because it affects both adolescents and the specially gifted, but also because I suspect that much of the recent discussion of these two topics may be a manifestation of our general uncertainty as to how best to proceed in the face of so many difficult problems. This widespread interest in our youth and specially gifted (creative) people may reflect the hope that at least they will be able to divert and entertain us and, at best, will come up with solutions to problems with which we feel we cannot deal adequately.

On Adolescence

In the Shorter Oxford English Dictionary adolescence is defined as 'the process or condition of growing up; the period between childhood and maturity'. It may help us to understand out subject if we digress briefly to consider some aspects of 'maturity'.

The goal of adolescence is the attainment of adulthood in all its aspects. These are physical (sexual, procreative and aggressive potency), cognitive, social (including spiritual and moral) attributes. Maturity here implies separation from, and independence of, the nurturing family that was needed during childhood. The capacity for deliberation before action and for reality-testing are other attributes of the maturing adolescent and the adult.

It could be said that a healthy adolescent or adult has kept alive within himself all of his own antecedent phases of development. Thus a mature adult can meet a child on the child's own terms—an age-appropriate way of responding to the child, since it presents the outer world to him in such a way that it can meaningfully become incorporated into his inner world. The child thus responded to, will in his turn grow confident in himself and become an adolescent and an adult able to be sympathetically responsive to the needs of others and so to contribute towards that creativity which is part of the universal nutrient substance of human life.

There is plenty of evidence that psychosocially many people grow steadily and evenly throughout adolescence. Nonetheless, in the literature,[9] a picture of a mythical adolescent emerges who is either in turmoil or someone 'struggling through the doldrums', for whom 'the cure is the passage of time',[10] of whom we may 'always expect the unexpected'. For adolescence is described as 'a time when too much is happening'[11] and is 'as definitely characterised

147

by domestic explosions and rebellion as typhoid is marked by fever'.[12]

Although in some cases there may be quantitative or qualitative changes in instinctual drives (sexual and aggressive) which are related to puberty and which may or may not be accompanied by the changes in mood or behaviour so often described in the literature on adolescence,[13] I think that most of the behaviour which is designated as 'typical' of adolescence occurs only under the following conditions or combinations of them:

1. If the physical changes of puberty are early or late relative to the peer group; or if there are marked inequalities of ability within such a peer group; or rivalry;

2. If the resolution of conflicts or traumas of earlier developmental stages has not been adequate, they will become reactivated in early adolescence. (Blos[14] called this the 'second phase of individuation'.); and

3. If society puts stress on the adolescent at that point[14, 15] for example, if parents have problems, or if pathological mourning processes are present in the family, or if a new sibling is born at this stage, or if there are economic pressures, etc.

Margaret Mead[15] considers adolescence 'the great period of personality, a function of the complexity of society, not merely the human life-cycle'. Erikson discussed this interrelationship at length in *Identity and the Life Cycle*.[16]

Because of his physical growth an adolescent is faced with the fact that he cannot and will not be handled by the adult world in the way in which he was handled during childhood, because the expression of his sexuality, aggression, or self-assertion can have real and permanent consequences. So adolescents have to prepare to assume personal responsibility for their dealings with their own inner standards[16] and with other people.

In our society adolescence is the time when young people move away from their immediate family into the wider world. Both adolescents and their parents suffer from problems related to separating, which run as an undercurrent affecting their relationship. Each group may at times express some form of protest or despair, or affect some form of detachment.

Our adolescents are not just a generation created by the media or marketing men, nor are they a generation created to remove the threat of unemployment from their elders—in terms of the overall culture which exists beyond the family; these adolescents are part of a most necessary longer period of dependence and nurture. They have to make sense of a constantly diverging and changing world. By examining our present age we may be able to understand why creativity and adolescence have become topics of such interest.

A Comment on Our Contemporary Society

Over-stimulation has become a disease of our times. As far as possible everyone maintains his personal equilibrium by exposing himself to whatever 'dose' of stimulation best suits him. Where people can no longer determine the amount of stimulation that they receive, whether by excessive stimulation or sensory deprivation, personality disintegration can result.

Over-stimulation is dealt with in various ways from cut-out mechanisms leading to feelings of boredom, even sleep[17] to the forced development of intellect, perhaps at the expense of other facets of the human personality. This disproportionate intellectual growth (or an ego distortion resulting in what Winnicott described as 'false self development')[18] may occur in individuals who are spurred to great efforts to cope with a rapidly changing, constantly impinging environment. Such individuals may be highly gifted, yet may readily lose their equilibrium or their sense of wholeness and continuity of being. They frequently complain of feeling alienated from themselves or from the world, and, perhaps because of their well-developed intellects, may attempt to integrate themselves by creative expression. The built-in over-stimulation in our society may lead some young people

149

to subject themselves to compulsive television watching or hi-fi noise input, that is, self-inflicted noise-bombardment. Conversely they seek alternative ways of life such as mystical religions, or turn to drugs, etc. It seems that we need to feel that someone, somewhere will surely be able to cope with and integrate this over-bombardment with people, noise, urgent issues and information which we suffer in our times. Thus there are revivals of interest in religious and in political ideologies, and, in the sociological and psychological fields, in our adolescents and the highly gifted.

Our society is at times described in terms similar to adolescence: 'Everything is changing relentlessly, abruptly and unpredictably. Shapes, values, landscapes, adulations, views, moods, opinions, fashions are on the non-stop move, as if a pitiless assembly-line were moving through our lives . . . one element of existence remains the same all the way. It's change itself.'[19] At the steep exponential rate of change from which society suffers, one way to adapt is to perpetuate a kind of adolescence. There may be a resistance to assuming a well-crystallised personality or identity when personal adaptability of role may appear to have greater survival value in such a situation as our current one, where a variety of dangers are predicted.

Mankind is suffering acutely from problems of wastage, maldevelopment of resources, misuse and non-use of knowledge and skills. We are in doubt as to how to behave at a time when our technological expertise, our collective self-awareness and self-reliance make behavioural choices necessary. On this planet man has proliferated and disruped ecological balance. How we act determines the quality of life now and in the future. Our youth cannot fail to be aware of this; anxiety, doubt, frustration, impotence, feelings of non-involvement (alienation), of helplessness and hopelessness beset the aware; optimists can only be tentative.

Yet the twentieth century is unique in offering to men for the first time both the opportunity and the means to fashion a social life according to their desires. It is for that reason both hopeful and terrible.[19] How are we, our youth, and the gifted in our midst to meet the challenges of our adolescent human state?

What Is It that Drives Someone to Be Specially Creatively Productive?

We don't know. The psychoanalytic and general literature on the topic of the creative process and motivation for creative productiveness is considerable but not always consistent in outlook. I have listed some articles of interest in the bibliography,[20] and some quotes which speak for themselves.[21] However, true genius remains inexplicable, perhaps a 'gift of the gods'.

Some scientists produce more under stress, others collapse. Some need quiet, some do not. Rivalry and predatoriness and competitiveness suit some, not others. Much of the work of the experimental psychologists is contradictory and confusing. They have attempted to assess creativity by measuring such factors as novelty of response, toleration of ambiguity, humour, etc.—that is, divergent thinking. Hudson[22,23] has demonstrated that it is not divergence or convergence, the style of thinking, which determines creative ability, but other factors, personality and personal history. Indeed, it is quite possible that it is psychic trauma (exposure to an 'overdose' of environmental stress beyond the coping capacity of the developing individual) suffered in childhood which is the starting point for the will and need to be productive in expressing creative ability later in life.

Creativity is expressed at all ages. The scribbled drawing of a child or the poem of an adolescent can have value from the standpoint of the individual, the function which this organised act of creation served at that time in expressing and maintaining that particular individual's integrity of personality. Objectively, such a product can be evaluated in relation to the degree of developmental maturity attained by that individual. But when an artefact is judged from a supra-individual perspective, that is in relation to our collective pooled and available consciousness, its value will obviously be very different. And even if it was a valuable contribution at the time it was produced (say, for example, some architectural plan or helpful project in the domain of science or dance or whatever), the question as to whether such creativity will contribute to our common human heritage, the non-genetic pool of works and ideas which carries evolution of our collective consciousness, is quite another matter.

Adolescence is not necessarily a period of special creative productivity: but from the point of view of the individual adolescent involved in creative effort *it is the positive value of the doing rather than the quality of the contribution that has to be recognised.*

The creative products of adolescence have been labelled 'also objects', substitutes for real ones.[23] There are a thousand ways of missing the bull's eye but only one of hitting it.[24] A considerable amount of adolescent creative effort falls into the 'miss' category viewed from the supra-individual perspective.

In his preface to 'Endymion', Keats[25] wrote: 'The imagination of a boy is healthy, and the mature imagination of a man is healthy, but there is a space of life between in which the soul is in a ferment, the character undecided, the way of life uncertain, the ambition thicksighted ... thence proceeds mawkishness.' Keats regarded this poem of his youth as a 'failure in a great object' denoting 'a feverish try rather than a deed accomplished', for his foundations were 'too sandy', the work itself evidence of inexperience and immaturity. In the eyes of history, such a judgement is the likely fate of most creative efforts of adolescents.

To utilise his talents in a productive way, an adolescent must be able to assert himself, to manage his sexuality, his aggressive and regressive drives, his love and his pain, and he must, of course, be able to express himself in a personal way. For his work to be of supra-individual value, he must also have developed mature cognitive powers, acquired maturity of judgement, steadiness of purpose and expertise. In other words, the personal psychodevelopmental tasks of adolescence have to be resolved or at least not stressing the adolescent too acutely if he is to make full use of his abilities.

Whilst some adolescents are capable of sustained concentration, other preoccupations of that period may produce conflict. Whilst for some individuals adolescence may be a time of special creative productivity, the products of such adolescents are rarely of anything other than individual significance.

How Are the Specially Gifted Described?

Specially gifted creative people are said[26] to be more likely than others to view authority as conventional rather than absolute; to make fewer black and white distinctions; to have a less dogmatic and more relativistic view of life; to show more independence of judgement; to be less conventional and conforming in behaviour both intellectual and social; to be more willing to entertain and sometimes to express their own 'irrational impulses', to place a greater value on humour and, in fact, to have a better sense of humour; in short, to be freer and somewhat less rigidly controlled than 'non-creatives'. Creative people tend to free themselves from a stimulus and use it largely as a point of departure for self-expression. The highly creatively gifted adolescent is said to have a more playful or, if you will, a more experimental attitude towards conventional ideas, objects and qualities.[27]

Highly productive creative people experience a series of adolescent-like crises, changed fields of interest, concentration and livelihood in their lives.[28] They ask questions with some urgency and have a sense of being separate and special, with special gifts which they handle differently.

Many gifted youngsters are 'well-adjusted socially, and neither pose nor experience much adolescent stress'. Nonetheless it seems generally agreed that owing to their unconventionality, independence of thought, and impulsiveness, creative or rather potentially creative productive people often run foul of authority in the social, occupational and educational realms, and may experience adolescent stress.

What Problems Do Gifted Adolescents Pose, and What Problems Do They Experience?

Children who have the need to be creative are most likely to get into conflict with authority. This is not surprising if we remember that if this creative potential is to become actualised they may be predatory, assertive and competitive. In the words of Faulkner,[21] 'The good artist believes that nobody is good enough to give him advice. He has supreme vanity. No matter how much he admires the old writer he wants to beat him.' No wonder very bright, very gifted children often experience their adolescent conflicts with authority figures in particularly acute fashion.

Many of our youth are better educated than their elders.[29] The gifted can think up many things that are difficult for the teachers to cope with. And teachers and parents, no less than youth, are confronted by general cultural problems. In addition, parents and teachers have to cope with ageing, perhaps with failure, with their envy of the young, probably with *not* being able to cope, and so on.

How May Creativity (health) and Special Talents and Ability Be Fostered during Adolescence? Can We Provide Our Gifted Adolescents with an Optimum Nurturing Environment? What Are the Optimal Conditions of Stress and Acceptance, Challenge and Tolerance, that Can Allow Them to Express Themselves and Fully Utilise Their Capacities?—

'To give a fair chance to potential creativity is a matter of life and death for any society. This is all-important, because the outstanding creative ability of a fairly small percentage of the population is mankind's ultimate capital asset, and the only one with which Man has been endowed.'[30]

Different situations facilitate productivity in different children or individuals. We do not know what is best for whom, or when or how. To pressurise an adolescent to express his ability can be counter-productive, even dangerous. Yet there is no evidence that a permissive classroom is more sound than one which frustrates the youngster and throws him back on his own thoughts.[22] The gifted, as much

154

as those less gifted, require encouragement. Every adolescent needs someone to keep his personal welfare in focus. All gifted and productive scientists and artists stress the personal significance of a close relationship to some older person during their adolescence who had encouraged them in their drive to question and produce answers to their questions.[28] Everyone, the gifted not excepted, relies on others in the world in which he is working to help him keep going. Peers can also help or hinder: the peer group is of course most important in adolescence.[31]

Only when he emerges from the safety of the familiar conventions and traditions of whatever rituals that child has created or encountered in a particular family is that child free to play, to explore, to create. Only when he emerges from the safety of the familiar can a child venture forth to explore and create a wider dimension of the world.

How much the nature of the relationship to one's parents influences one creative attitudes, and to what extent those creative attitudes may be isolated from the personal parts of life, is questionable.[32]

If a gifted adolescent suffers fears of passivity associated with the idea of castration, the result may be that the development of creative capability may become unacceptable and be warded off as dangerous. Alternatively, such fears may be rationalised, for example, into an active religious experience. In either case there is the possibility of sacrifice or distortion of creative work.

Under-achieving gifted adolescents are able themselves to delineate some of their deep-seated personality problems. However, a personality problem can only be viewed in relation to the environment with which the individual is dealing. Even if high ability is present, a productive and gifted adolescent may not be able to manage his environmental pressures in such a way that his talents may be expressed. We must be on the alert to detect problems early and try to enable adolescents to resolve them.

What is a parent or teacher to do? The answer, as usual, is to assess each case on its individual merits. Perhaps we could hold in mind Thoreau's words: 'I would not have anyone adopt my mode of living on any account: for, besides that, before he has fairly learnt it, I may have found another for myself. I desire that there may be as many different persons in the world as possible, but I would have each one very careful to find out and pursue his own way . . .'[33]

Winnicott said, 'We cannot meet our adolescents with the words "over to you". Not only in infancy and childhood but also in adolescence we have to provide the facilitating environment in which each person may grow and find values in which he can believe. By the time the child is growing towards an adult state the accent is no longer on the moral code: it must pass over to that more positive thing, the storehouse of man's cultural achievement.'[34]

Bearing in mind that, 'most important (is) the need to keep human development open for the realisation of new possibilities',[4] what more can we do? We can question both our goals and our means today,[35] in other words, what we aim at in education and the way in which we try to educate our youth.[40]

We need people who can teach their children not *what* to learn but *how* to learn, not *what* they *should* be committed to, but the *value* of commitment. Mead[29] suggests that in the future we must move towards the creation of open systems that focus on children whose capacities are least known, and whose choices must be left open rather than, as in the past, where the focus was on the individual and those who had learnt the most and were able to do the most with what they had learnt.

Indeed we must question our educational system which Ivan Illich[36] has designated our current 'sacred cow'. He calls for institutional revolution, a deschooling of society. Although they adopt extreme postions, writers like Illich and Goodman[37] present a point of view which those who deal with the gifted, and indeed, all our young, would do well to consider carefully. Education is a large industry at present.[38] Teachers and parents are devoted to maintaining their institutions of learning, and such institutions do not easily contain students who are original, who lack suggestibility, and tolerate ambiguity and structural disorderliness.

'Indirectness marks all creative expression',[39] but this is not always praiseworthy in the eyes of teachers.

Neither an artist nor a scientist who is a creator can drop his work and have it taken up by another without doing it violence. Current academic programmes do not generally cater for work of this kind done by gifted adolescents. It is not the thing done or made which is necessarily beautiful, but the doing. Bronowski[5] considers beauty 'the by-product of interest and pleasure in the choice of action'. Were teachers to recognise that a gifted man cannot handle anything without taking fire from what he does and having his emotions engaged, they might better facilitate the interests of the young with whom they work.

Concluding Remarks

However beguiling it is to *read* about creativity and adolescence, it is perhaps spurious to point out that to do so is to escape from experiencing either. Neither exists outside the changing landscape of human societies in their manifold times and places. Both are episodic yet timeless, universal but nonetheless unique. Both processes are highly personal, natural and inescapable aspects of being alive, responsive and human. Not everyone achieves the full experience of either state. Both are topics currently charged with interest. For those who seek that aspect, they will find that both are topics about people rich in conflict and paradox. Both processes seem at times mysterious; both are earnestly studied, much described, sometimes disturbing, often satisfying, frequently envied, restless attempts to reshape our social world.

'Nature puts no question and answers none that we mortals ask.'[33] But man, the questioner, as Robert Motherwell wrote,[41] 'is his own invention; every artist's problem is to invent himself'. And that is the task of every adolescent, and every adolescent is every man.

The process of adolescence is also part of the progress of sentience and sensibility in the adolescent task of coming to terms with illusion, with disillusion and with transience; this too requires creative effort. Each of us achieves some personal adaptive equilibrium, precarious or otherwise; collectively we rely on the gifted among us to sport with, to balance or even perhaps (in the case of the efforts of those who achieve works of genius) to reach beyond the forces of entropy to which we all finally succumb. Thus the evolution of consciousness proceeds, midst the ebb and flow of the times.

NOTES, REFERENCES AND ADDITIONAL READING

1. In a thoughtful and scathing review, 'Only God Can Make a Tree – But We Can Measure Creativity' (*Psychiatry and Social Science Review*, Vol. 4, No. 6, pp. 25–31), reviewing Frank Barron, *Creative Person and Creative Process* (New York, Holt, Reinhart & Winston, 1969), N. Herman points out that we now have a branch of academic psychology whose province is creativity. It has come of age with institutions, conferences, and journals of creative behaviour with proliferating biographical apparatus. In 1963, 4,176 items were listed on creative imagination (cf. 185 items in Psychological Abstracts in 1950) in the bibliography of the Creative Foundation, and by now surely more than thrice that number are listed. Susan M. Stievater has compiled a bibliography which represents several hundred recent books on creativity and problem solving, and is incomplete! Liam Hudson sums up: 'Creativity as a topic for research represents a boon in the American psychological industry, only paralleled by that of programmed learning.'

2. A mind that is everywhere is nowhere: creativity begins with exclusion and arrests with focus. Thus are revealed new aspects of reality, new problems to engage the perceptive. Reality is that which is ever beyond the grasp of that with which we grope. As we reach towards it, it recedes. Now we are running as fast as the mirage that is the vision that seems within our grasp.

3. Ontogeny recapitulates phylogeny: each man in his own development goes through stages analogous to those postulated for the evolution of Man. In *The Naked Ape* (Harmondsworth, Penguin Books, 1970) Desmond Morris suggests that man's absolute dependence on the nurturing parental environment during infancy is a necessary evolutionary phase which permitted the development of the capacity for symbolic communication (language).

4. Part of the awesome process of energy-transformation which occurs in the matter of our human bodies is that which eventually results in the realm of our creativity. Part of this creative productivity becomes manifest in shared communications, the evolving mind of collective mankind, called the *noosphere* by Pierre Teilhard de Chardin (*The Phenomenon of Man*, and *The Future of Man*, Lon-

don, Collins, 1964). Inexorable has been the growth of this 'storehouse of man's cultural achievement', (D. W. Winnicott, *Playing and Reality*, London, Tavistock, 1971), the environment which only human life inhabits and explores, where 'the communication of the dead is tongued with fire beyond the language of the living' (T. S. Eliot, 'Little Gidding', *Four Quartets*, London, Faber & Faber, 1944). 'Properly developed human personalities are the highest products of evolution. They have greater capacities, and have reached a higher level of organisation than any other part of the world's substance.' (Julian Huxley, *Evolution in Action*, Harmondsworth, Penguin Books, and London, Chatto & Windus, 1951).

5. 'A rational aesthetic must start from the conviction that art (and science too) is a normal activity of human life.' (Jacob Bronowski, 'The Creative Process', *Creativity: A Discussion* at the Nobel Conference organised by Gustavus Adolphus College, St Peter, Minnesota, Jan. 1970; ed. by John D. Roslansky, London, North-Holland Publishing Co.; New York, Fleet Academics Editors Inc.) pp. 17–32. Chomsky asserts that the potential for creative understanding and use of literature is innate (John Lyons, *Chomsky*, London, Fontana Collins, 1970).

Faulkner:[21] 'If I had not existed someone else would have written me, Hemingway, Dostoevsky, all of us. For what is important is the Shakespearian plays, not who wrote them, but that somebody did. The artist is of no importance. Only what he creates is of importance since there is nothing new to be said.'

'No intellect, no ardour is redundant: to make one through the other more abundant is what we're for. . . .' (Rainer Maria Rilke, *Selected Poems*, Harmondsworth Penguin Books, 1972).

6. See Erik Erikson, *Identity and the Life Cycle* (New York, International University Press, 1959). C. P. Snow emphasises this point: 'We are not going to turn out men and women today who understand as much of our world as Piero della Francesca did of his, or Pascal or Goethe. With good fortune, however, we can educate a large proportion of our better minds so that they are not ignorant of imaginative experience of applied science, nor ignorant either of the endowments of applied science, of the remediable suffering of most of their fellow humans and of the responsibilities which, once they are seen, cannot be denied. In a world in which we have to make do in our half-educated fashion, struggling to hear messages, as though listening to a foreign language of which one knows only a few words, obviously a long period of education is a necessity' (*Two Cultures*, and *Second Look*, Cambridge University Press, 1964).

7. D. W. Winnicott, *The Child, the Family and the Outside World* (Harmondsworth, Penguin Books, 1969); *The Family and Individual Development* (London, Tavistock, 1965).

8. D. W. Winnicott, *Playing and Reality* (London, Tavistock, 1971).

9. Norman O. Kiell, *The Universal Experience of Adolescence* (New York, International University Press, 1964); and *Adolescence Through Fiction* (New York, International University Press, 1959).

10. D. W. Winnicott, 'Adolescence: Struggling through the Doldrums', *The Family and Individual Development* (London, Tavistock, 1964).

11. Bruno Bettelheim, *Symbolic Wounds* (London, Thames & Hudson, 1955).

12. Ruth Benedict, quoted by Norman O. Kiell.[9]

13. *On Adolescence*
    D. W. Winnicott, 'Adolescence and the Need for Personal Confrontation', *Paediatrics*, Vol. 44, No. 5, pp. 752–6; 'Youth Will not Sleep', *New Society*, Vol. 1 (28 May, 1964).
    Derek Miller, *The Age Between* (London, Cornmarket/Hutchinson, 1969); and 'Youth, Creativity and Rebellion', *New Society* (1968).
    Erik Erikson, *Ego Development and Historical Change* (Psychological Issues, 1959); and *Childhood and Society* (Harmondsworth, Penguin Books, 1969).
    L. A. Spiegel, 'Comments on the Psychoanalytic Psychology of Adolescence', in *Psycho-Analytic Study of the Child*, Vol. 13 (New York, International University Press, 1958).
    Raymond Kuhlen, *The Psychology of Adolescent Development* (New York, Harper, 1952).
    G. Stanley Hall, *Adolescence: Its Psychology and its Relationship to Physiology, Anthropology, Sociology, Sex, Crime, Religion and Education* (New York, Appleton Century Crofts, 1904) – started the bias towards describing adolescence as a period of turmoil etc.

14. Peter Blos, *On Adolescence* (New York, Free Press, 1962); and 'Adolescence: The Second Phase of Individuation', *Psycho-Analytic Study of the Child*, Vol. 12 (New York, International University Press, 1967).

15. Margaret Mead, 'Adolescents in Primitive and Modern Society', *Readings in Social Psychology* (New York, Holt, Rinehart & Winston, 1947).

16. Erik Erikson, 'The Roots of Virtue', *The Humanist Frame*, Julian Huxley (ed.) (London, George Allen & Unwin, 1961).

17. Ian Oswald, *Sleep* (Harmondsworth, Penguin Books, 1966).

18. D. W. Winnicott, 'Ego Distortion in Terms of True and False Self' (1960); and 'Classification: Is There a Psycho-Analytic Contribution to Psychiatric Classification? (1959, *The Maturational Processes and the Facilitating Environment* (London, Hogarth Press, 1965).

19. Leopold Tyrmand, 'Nine Mini-Treatises on America: A New York Notebook', *Encounter* (Feb. 1972), p. 58.

20. *On Creativity*
    J. W. Getzels and P. W. Jackson, *The Study of Giftedness: A Multidimensional Approach* (Abnormal & Soc. Psychology, Vol. 61, July 1960), pp. 119–23.

J. Henry, 'Working Paper on Creativity', *Harvard Educational Review*, No. 27 (Spring 1957), pp. 148–55.

Ernest Jones, 'Nature of Genius', *Scientific Monthly*, No. 81 (Feb. 1957).

Harold H. Anderson. *Creativity in Childhood and Adolescence: A Diversity of Approaches* (Scientific and Behavioural Books Inc., Palo Alto, Calif., 1965).

Anthony Storr, *The Dynamics of Creation* (London, Secker & Warburg, 1972).

Mora Tywon, 'Creativity' in *New Horizons in Psychology*, Brian M. Foss (ed.) (Penguin Books, 1966).

Marion Milner, Appendix to *On Not Being Able to Paint*, London, Heinemann Educational Books Ltd, (HEB paperback edn, 1971).

David Holbrook, 'The Wizard and the Critical Flame: Implications about Moral Growth from the Works of Donald Winnicott', *Psychiatry and Social Science Review*, Vol. 4, No. 6 (12 May, 1970), pp. 2–16.

Silvano Arieti, 'Creativity and Its Cultivation', *American Handbook of Psychiatry*, Vol. 3 (New York, Basic Books, 1968).

Arthur Koestler, *The Act of Creation* (London, Pan Books, 1964; Danube edn 1970).

Gilbert J. Rose, *Narcisstic Fusion States and Creativity in the Unconscious Today*, Mark Kanzer (ed.) (New York, International University Press, 1971).

J. E. Drevdahl, 'Factors of Importance for Creativity', *Journal of Clinical Psychology*, Vol. 12 (Jan. 1956), pp. 21–6.

21. 'The artist requires 99 per cent talent, 99 per cent discipline, 99 per cent work. He must never be satisfied with what he does. He has a dream. It anguishes him so much he must get rid of it. He has no peace until then. Everything goes by the board: honour, pride, decency, security, happiness, all to get the book written. Art has no concern with peace of mind.'

'The artist is a creature driven by demons. He don't know why they choose him, and he is usually too busy to wonder why.' (William Faulkner, *Writers at Work: Selections from Paris Review*: interviews by Kay Dick, Harmondsworth, Penguin Books, 1972).

Aaron Copland in *Music and Imagination* (Harmondsworth, Penguin Books, 1970) says: 'The more I live the life of music, the more I am convinced that it is the freely imaginative mind that is at the core of all vital music-making and music-listening. An imaginative mind is essential to the creation of art in any medium ... human travail enters into every creation.'

Sigmund Freud to Ernest Jones, edited and selected by Benjamin Nelson (*Freud and the Twentieth Century*, London, Allen & Unwin, 1958) said: 'Creative imagination and work go together with me: I take no delight in anything else. That would be a prescription for happiness were it not for the terrible thought that one's productivity depended on sensitive moods.'

Donald Woods Winnicott: 'It is creative apperception more than anything else that makes the individual feel that life is worth living ... our theory includes a belief that living creatively is a healthy state.'[4]

22. Liam Hudson, *Contrary Imaginations: A Psychological Study of the English Schoolboy* (London, Methuen, 1966; Harmondsworth, Penguin Books, 1967); and *Frames of Mind: Ability, Perception and Self-Perception in the Arts and Sciences* (London, Methuen, 1968; Harmondsworth, Penguin Books, 1970).

23. Bernfield, quoted by Blos.[14]

24. Michel de Montaigne, *Essays on Literature and Learning*, J. M. Cohen (trans.) (London, Secker & Warburg, 1966; Harmondsworth, Penguin Books, 1967) p. 89.

25. John Keats, *Keats' Poetical Works*, H. W. Garrod (ed.) (Oxford University Press, 1970).

26. Bernard Berelson and G. A. Steiner, *Human Behaviour, an Inventory of Scientific Findings* (New York, Harcourt Brace Books Inc., 1964).

27. J. W. Getzels and P. W. Jackson, *Creativity and Intelligence* (New York, Wiley, 1962).

28. Snyder and Tessman, 'Creativity', *Gifted Students and Scientists*. A discussion at the Nobel Conference organised by Gustavus Adolphus College, St. Peter, Minnesota, Jan. 1970. Ed. by John D. Roslansky (London, North-Holland Publishing Co.; New York, Fleet Academic Editions Inc.) p. 19.

29. Margaret Mead, 'Gifted Children in the American Culture of Today', *Journal of Teacher Education*, Vol. 5 (1954), pp. 211–14, and *Culture and Commitment* (London, Bodley Head, 1970).

30. Harold Toynbee, 'Is America Neglecting Her Creative Minority?' *Widening Horizons in Creativity*, Calvin W. Taylor (ed.), The Proceedings of the Fifth Utah Creativity Research Conference 1964 (New York and London, John Wylie & Sons Inc.) p. 4.

31. P. Willmott, *Adolescent Boys of East London* (London, Routledge & Kegan Paul, 1966).

32. Phyllis Greenacre, 'The Childhood of the Artist' *Psycho-Analytic Study of the Child*, Vol. 12 (1957) pp. 47–53; 'Libidinal Phase Development and Giftedness', *Psycho-Analytic Study of the Child*, Vol. 12 (1959); 'Discussion and Comments on the Psychology of Creativity', *Journal of American Academy Child Psychiatry*, Vol. 1 (1962), pp. 129–37.

33. Henry David Thoreau, *Walden* (Viking, Portabie Thoreau, Viking Press, New York).

34. Donald Woods Winnicott, 'Morals and Education', *The Maturation Process and the Facilitating Environment* (London, Hogarth Press, 1965), pp. 93–108.

35. 'Ours is a civilisation committed to the quest for continually im-

proved means and to carelessly examined ends. Since the religious object is that which is uncritically worshipped, technology tends more and more to become the new god.' (Jacques Ellul, *The Technological Society*, John Wilkinson (trans.), London, Vintage Books, 1973).

36. Ivan D. Illich, *Deschooling Society* (London, Calder & Boyars, 1971); *A Celebration of Awareness* (London, Calder & Boyars, 1972).

37. Paul Goodman, *People or Personnel*, and *Like a Conquered Province* (New York, Vintage Books, 1957).

38. Peter Drucker, *The Age of Discontinuity*: *Guidelines to our Changing Society* (London, Pan Books, 1971).

39. Stanley Burnshaw, *The Seamless Web* (Allen Lane, The Penguin Press, 1970).

40. *Further Reading On Education*

    G. A. Lyward, 'Parents and Public School', *Home and School* (March, 1970).

    A. H. Passon, 'Identifying and Counselling the Gifted College Students', *Journal of Higher Education*, Vol. 28 (Jan. 1957), pp. 21–9.

    R. J. Havighurst, 'Conditions Favourable and Detrimental to the Development of Talent', *School Review*, Vol. 65 (March 1957), pp. 20–6.

    L. Feln, 'Learning is Aggressive: Case Study of Analysis of the Defence Against Learning in Underachieving Gifted Children', *Gifted Child*, Vol. 2 (Spring 1958), pp. 34–6.

    J. C. Gowan, *An Annotated Bibliography of the Academically Talented* (1961); (ed.) *Educating Gifted Children: A Book of Readings* (New York, Holt & Co., 1959), pp. 480–9.

    G. D. Maybee and L. L. Myers, 'How Can the Junior High School Provide for the Academically Talented Student?' *Bulletin of the National Association of Secondary School Principals*, Vol. 43 (April 1959), pp. 19–23.

    R. D. McCurdy, 'Characteristics and Backgrounds of Superior Science Students', *School Review*, No. 64 (Feb. 1956), pp. 67–71.

    C. P. Snow comments, 'In our society (that is advanced Western Society) we have lost even the pretence of a common culture. Persons educated with the greatest intensity we know can no longer communicate with each other on the plane of their major intellectual concern. This is serious for our creative, intellectual, and above all, our moral life. It is leading us to interpret the past wrongly, to misjudge the present, and to deny our hopes of the future. It is making it difficult or impossible for us to take good action.'[6]

    'The principal goal of education is to create men who are capable of doing new things, not simply of repeating what other generations have done – men who are creative, inventive and discoverers. . . . The truth is there are no absolute truths, all is merely creation. . . .

A faith, a strong belief sustained and repeated can give birth to reality.' (Jean Piaget quoted by David Elkind in *Children and Adolescents: Interpretive Essays on Jean Piaget*, Oxford University Press, 1970).

'It has been shown that there may be 500 times difference in the rate of speed of learning in any one classroom. The reader can draw his own implications.'

41. Frank O'Hara, *Robert Motherwell* (The Museum of Modern Art, New York, distributed by Doubleday & Co., 1959).

10

Adolescents and Groups Subcultures Countercultures

PAUL UPSON

Introduction

It is by now a commonplace to say that every adolescent passes through an acute and sometimes chronic identity crisis. However, as soon as we pause to consider what constitutes a successful negotiation of this crisis stage in development, the arguments start; and this of course is essentially because, in the final analysis, and at the deepest level, every adolescent must eventually move towards the acceptance of a moral and ethical code, a system of values, by which he decides to live out his life as an adult.

It is hardly surprising, therefore, that the terms 'positive' and 'negative' identity should have been coined by Erikson in the effort to indicate whether the system of attitudes, beliefs, standards, and ideals towards which the adolescent seems to be moving is roughly in accord with the prevailing value system of the society in which he lives. Although social scientists in general go out of their way to maintain that they take a wholly dispassionate, impersonal, and objective stance towards the phenomena they are studying, it is as well to keep in mind at the outset that psychiatry at any rate, and

165

perhaps even more so the esoteric world of psychoanalysis, have very clear ideas about what constitutes a 'productive' and 'fulfilling' life for the individual. We should not forget that however arbitrary a value system is seen to be in theory, once embraced by large numbers of people in practice, it rapidly assumes the status of a creed. The authoritarianism of the left is not, unfortunately, a figment in the imagination of the right.

But, rather than getting involved in tedious philosophical discussions about whether absolute criteria can be applied to the life style 'chosen' by any particular individual, it might be more helpful to consider just why there is such an exclusive concern in the literature, not to say the mass media, with what are taken as 'negative' life styles pursued by adolescents depicted as forever trapped in their 'negative' identities. The usual answer to this question is that society is made so desperately anxious and afraid by the 'negative' goings-on in its midst that it neglects altogether the 'positive' good works carried out by adolescents—a teenage mugging rates the headlines, the raising of £500 for charity only three lines at the foot of the page, if at all. But the view that I shall take in this chapter is that adolescence, if nothing else, is a time of the most desperate extremes; and yet, paradoxically, if we allow ourselves to become preoccupied either with one extreme or the other, we fall into the same mental trap that is set for all adolescents. Life becomes, for a time at any rate, a constant shuttling back and forth between any number of extremes; whilst the adult world strives frantically to see a pattern in, to make sense of, indeed to inject some sanity into, these apparently absurd contradictions. But it is only when we can stop being overwhelmed by the extremity of the extremes themselves that we can perhaps begin to see how we might help the adolescent towards some point in the middleground between them.

Although I have spoken of a number of extremes, at the risk of being accused of applying the familiar reductionist argument so beloved of the psychoanalytic world, I would like to suggest that they are all versions of the basic good / bad dichotomy into which the newborn infant splits his earliest experiences of the world. In the context of this chapter, it perhaps makes most sense to think of this dichotomy in terms of the creative as opposed to the destructive potential which every adolescent is only too well aware he has inside him. It would be no exaggeration (since adolescence is a time of exaggeration) to say that through the mind of every adolescent, frightened and yet excited by the final stages in the development and maturation of his mental and physical powers and equipment, there flashes again and again the almost overwhelming message: 'Now *anything* is possible', to be followed immediately by the nagging doubt, 'Or is it?'

Every intelligent adolescent has by now grasped the insistent message put across by the social scientists that there is nothing sacred or absolute in the way in which any society organises itself, but only the successful imposition of a value system on the whole of society by a part of it (usually of course the largest part). We should hardly be surprised, therefore, that many adolescents today seek to establish not merely their own (as we see it) 'peculiar' identities with which to cock a snoop at our value system, not merely their own particular version of how life could and should be led ('for a while' as we again like to see it), but a subculture which they may well see as a rival and a counter to the one which prevails amongst the majority.

Thus the question of what Erikson would call an 'ideological commitment' becomes of paramount importance. It is precisely because, as the adolescent sees it, the possibilities are limitless in either direction, for 'good' or for 'evil', that the idealism of youth is always balanced by its nihilism or anarchism (the destruction of all ideals), and that society's acceptance of change is balanced, as always, by its inherent conservatism. And, yet, if the energies of youth cannot be channelled, whether for 'constructive' (the Peace Corps?) or 'destructive' (the war in Vietnam?) purposes, then indeed no kind of change, for 'better' (progress?) or 'worse' (subversion?) will ever occur.

I should like to start off a discussion of some of these

issues by considering in some detail the case history of a young man I saw for psychological testing.

Nick was a sixteen-year-old 'drop-out' who, despite an IQ well within the very superior range, had left school at fifteen without taking any exams because, as he put it: 'I didn't agree with the exam system.' He had left home at the same time (he was an only child) and gone to live in the house of a schoolfriend whose parents he professed to admire because they seemed 'with it', held 'wild' parties, etc. His own parents he dismissed as being more interested in each other than in anyone else to the point of excluding him altogether from their lives. He described his new home as a 'commune', i.e. a place where traditional family values did not hold. He lived there for over a year, during which time he was introduced to drugs, in particular LSD, and also came to the attention of the police. One day he decided to use a PO mail sack he had found, to carry all his possessions in because he was 'going on the road', i.e. doing the opposite of the respectable surburban commuter. Needless to say, he got no further than the outskirts of London before he was stopped by the police and charged with stealing by finding a PO sack. (Found not guilty.) The second offence involved using a sword-stick to 'fence with a friend' outside a pub late one night, for which he was charged with possessing an offensive weapon. (Case dismissed.) Having successfully provoked those in authority on these two occasions, whilst managing to escape without punishment, he proceeded to commit a more serious offence whilst under the influence of drugs, namely, using the PO savings book of his friend's parents to try and obtain money from a post office. For this he was remanded on bail pending a psychiatric report.

Nick was tall, physically very well developed, and looked at least eighteen. His general attitude seemed to be one of almost manic denial that the authorities would come down on him heavily in the near future, coupled with an omnipotent determination to 'get a kick' out of it if they did. 'Whatever they give me, I will make the most of it, get what I can out of it.' He freely admitted using drugs, and said it was surprising he hadn't been caught by the police yet, though now he tried to be more careful about the whole business. However, in almost the same breath, he went on to say that he'd been letting off home-made bombs in the back garden of the commune where he now lived, and the last one had brought Scotland Yard racing along. When I suggested that he ran the risk, by his behaviour, of society and authority severely punishing him (i.e. confirming him in a 'negative' identity pattern); and that I thought that would be a waste of the talents and abilities he clearly had, he said: 'It's a shock to hear you putting it like that.' Yet he recovered almost immediately, and went on: 'I believe I'll get through to the other side. . . . When I get older and I do start on a new life, I will have a very successful one. . . . I won't be together till I'm eighteen at least, but I'm going to do OK. . . . Meanwhile I'm going to go on till I'm ready, and then make a positive start.' The notion of what Erikson would call the 'psycho-social moratorium', the compelling need of the adolescent to buy time, so to speak, in which to try and work out just what he has got to offer the adult world, is vividly expressed in these words.

Nick's stories to the pictures of the Object Relations Technique (a projective test which attempts to combine the advantages of both the Rorschach and the TAT) illustrate perfectly the battle going on inside him between what we might quite legitimately call, I think, the forces of good and evil. The story to the first picture, *A1*, the silhouette of a figure surrounded by a diffuse, almost enveloping foggy atmosphere, in which there are nevertheless vague possibilities for forming a relationship (a source of light, suggestion of an archway, a huddled human figure, etc.) runs as follows:

'Picture's being seen by a guy going blind. He worked in a chemical plant. There was an explosion. Chemicals got into his eyes, and he's going blind. Everything seems foggy, going very slowly foggy. . . . He sees person up in front of him. He's got laryngitis, going to ask him to help him to cross the road. But doesn't know there's a road between them. He walks across. It's a road without a pavement. A car shoots out and he's killed. . . . [Long pause] Wasn't way I intended to end it, but couldn't think of anything else. Was just going to go blind. . . . Of course I could have said knock on his body from the car changes his metabolism, and he recovers his sight.'

The 'touch and go' nature of this story, the preoccupation with which way things are going to turn out, whether for good or for evil, I think indicates only too clearly Nick's underlying anxiety and concern about which way his own life was going to turn out.

This deeply felt ambivalence about his own potential, whether it could be put to positive and constructive use, or whether he was destined to employ it in a negative and destructive manner, is vividly reflected in his story to the second card, *A2*, which depicts a man and a woman standing side by side in an obviously warm, close, and physical relationship, with, between them, a hint in the far distance of the world of reality beyond their intimacy. Nick says:

'A man and a woman, coming out of cave on the edge of the sea, wading into the sea. They seem very shy, like they're just coming together, wading over to an island. The island is their own. You can see the house on the island. They work hard. It's the Garden of Eden. . . . But that was Paradise, here they put a lot of work into it, and as much as they do, they'll get out of it, so it seems like Paradise. . . . But there will be a mistake. Like the universe is pure mathematics, but it can't be absolutely pure. That's impossible, there has to be some mistake somewhere. . . . So like the Garden of Eden they'll get thrown out into the sea, and turn into mermaids.'

Here the 'mistake', as in the Garden of Eden, is Nick's own awareness of the instinctual, and perhaps destructive, forces inside himself. When I put this to him, he summed up perfectly the battle going on in his inner world: 'No matter how constructive you are, there must be some destruction, but something constructive can come out of that. It's like a cosmic law.'

It is interesting to note that there were several stories in which the notion of retribution and punishment as vested in authority figures plays a very prominent part. It is as if Nick is saying that a part of him does realise that, sooner or later, limits *will* be set to his provocative behaviour, society *will* draw the line somewhere. Following a card to which he gave a violent story, Nick entered into a discussion with himself about whether physical violence could be justified in certain circumstances, and ended up talking about the Yin/Yang (Female/Male) dichotomy in ancient Chinese philosophy. His comment, 'Being yanged up is being ready to use violence', suggests strongly that we are still dealing with the basic (and by now I hope familiar) creative/destructive dichotomy; and he finally gave me what in a sense he knew was the only solution himself: 'You've got to achieve a perfect balance.'

Groups and Subcultures

The adolescent group to which Nick saw himself as owing at least temporary allegiance is largely distinguished by those who belong to it calling themselves 'freaks', whatever verbal labels might be applied to them by those whom they condemn as belonging to the 'straight' world. These terms, of course, belong essentially to the drug subculture, and their application is a very striking illustration of Erikson's reflection that nowadays many adolescents go out of their way to demonstrate that they are indeed going through an 'identity crisis', and want to make quite sure we know all about it. But every adolescent group attempts to draw its own boundaries, and thus establish its identity, by adopting its own particular (and often 'peculiar') habits and modes of behaviour: the way it dresses, the language it speaks, the places it frequents, the records it buys etc. This applies just as much to adolescent groups towards which society takes a 'positive' stance—the Girl Guides, the Peace Corps, Task Force—as to those against whom it reacts negatively—the Hells Angels, the Weathermen, and the Angry Brigade. Society is continually passing judgement on the adolescent groups. At best a group can be described as performing a

171

'valuable' function, or doing a 'worthwhile' job, because its behaviour is seen as helping to support (prop up?) the values which society holds so dear to its heart; at worst, its members can be described as 'dangerous fanatics' and their behaviour as 'subversive' because it is seen as posing a threat to society's very existence. What I believe to be of the most profound, not to say practical, importance, is to try to understand what we are doing when we distinguish between all these multifarious groups on the basis of whether or not their members are tending towards the establishment of a 'positive' or a 'negative' identity. Only then, I think, are we in a better position to grasp what is meant by the use of such terms as 'subculture' and 'counterculture'.

One of the things which should make us wary of labelling any adolescent group prematurely, is the sheer speed with which its defining characteristics can change overnight. A simple example from early adolescence which bears eloquent witness to this fact is the speed with which the idols of the 'teenybopper' world change. Pop groups themselves disband and reform under other names and different members with bewildering speed and complexity. In much the same fashion, their fans tear down from their walls pictures of their idols which they put up only a week ago. So the world of pop mirrors faithfully the frenetic world of early adolescence, and perhaps rightly, we dismiss such behaviour as 'fads' or 'phases' which will soon pass. In similar vein, we tend to treat lightly and play down the latest extremes of dress or language, largely because we are aware that such excesses, such deliberate and flamboyant attempts to be seen as different, reflect only the more superficial aspects of an adolescent 'life style'.

However, as we move on towards *middle* adolescence, such characteristics may begin to be associated with groups whose members society comes to view with increasing suspicion, because it believes they are moving towards the acceptance of certain attitudes (if not beliefs and ideals) which might offer a challenge to society's established way of life. Yet society is not quite sure, and correspondingly, we, as some of its representatives, should perhaps hesitate to speak yet of such groups as having an 'ideological commitment' (to use Erikson's phrase), since this does seem to imply a system of values which may pose some kind of threat to society's own.

There are an extremely large number of adolescent groups which arouse such ambivalent feelings in society, in the sense that it feels unable to pass off their behaviour as a 'phase' which will pass, yet is unwilling to condemn them outright. In a way we are saying that, like every parent of an adolescent, we live in hope that there will be a retreat from whatever extreme is currently engaging all their enthusiasm and energy. An example of what I am talking about on this side of the Atlantic would be the activities of a group of adolescents who, it seems, do not wish to be identified as 'heads', 'freaks', or 'hippies' (choose your own label one might say) with their long hair, exotic clothes, sandals or bare feet, and who therefore shave their heads, wear braces with dungarees or overalls, and large workmen's type boots. (It is not perhaps a coincidence that they come largely from the working class, whilst a good many 'heads' are middle-class student drop-outs.) Not surprisingly, they call themselves 'skinheads', and to make it clear that they do not share any commitment towards 'love' and 'peace' (certainly part of the ideology of the hippie movement across the world), they actively engage in hateful warring whenever they come across members of a group or subculture which they perceive as different, and perhaps threatening, to their own. An immigrant (or for that matter someone who supports a different football team) can fulfil this role just as easily as any 'head'. They also prefer pep pills and other stimulants which encourage direct action on the external world, whilst the 'heads' opt for drugs which encourage exploration of the inner world e.g. pot or LSD.

In this way these two groups seem to play out the opposite extremes of almost any dimension of behaviour one might care to name. As it happens, they are both somewhat towards the 'negative' end of the scale in so far as society is tempted to pass judgement on them, and this is not surprising, since the destructive aspects of their behaviour are so overt. Society is hardly likely to take a positive view of any group which threatens violence to innocent 'members of the public' and innocent property which gets in the way of the 'skinheads'. Similarly, it tends towards the view that the use and abuse of drugs is in the first place self-destructive; and may also lead to overt violence as a result of drugs or because of the need for large sums of money to obtain drug supplies.

But even the use of the term 'self-destructive' can lead us into dangerous territory, since we might argue that what it essentially refers to is the belief that the adolescent will not 'settle down' in the sense of contributing what skills and abilities he has within the social, political, and above all economic system that society has organised for itself. There is indeed a shared version of reality which most members of society cannot see as otherwise, and on which its value system is inevitably based. We have all gone through our individual struggles in coming to terms with it, i.e. we have learnt to be 'realistic'. Thus it is hardly surprising that perhaps the most typical accusation levelled at adolescents is that they are 'unrealistic'—which is only another way of saying that they still operate with the conviction, 'Now *any- thing* is possible.' But interestingly enough, although we started talking about the 'destructive' adolescent tending towards a 'negative' identity, we are now essentially talking about the 'constructive' indeed the 'idealistic' adolescent who is perhaps too 'positive' in his hopes and ambitions about what he can do in and for the world. It is important to realise that, although we do not read about it in the mass media, it can be just as painful for an adolescent to discover that his devoted efforts for Oxfam do not rid the world of starvation, as for a Weatherman or member of the Angry Brigade to discover that his bomb-making effort do not bring the world to its knees. In much the same way, although the activities of a Jesus freak or member of the Divine Light Mission (or for that matter, anyone with strong religious convictions) do not usually rate the headlines, and we have the nagging feeling 'After all, such young people are not actually doing any *harm* in the world, are they?' it can be just as difficult for them as for the convinced Marxist-Leninist to accept that the world does not necessarily buy their version of reality.

Thus although the term 'negative' identity is applied, by and large, to those who are seen as intent on destroying the system in one way or another, I think it is also true that an adolescent can have too *much* of a 'positive' identity in the sense of being hopelessly unrealistic about the constructive use to which his energies can be put. This should make it quite clear that the use of these terms is inextricably bound up with the version of reality which is accepted and shared by the majority.

It might be instructive to consider at this point those adolescents who by and large do come to accept the version of reality which is propounded by the 'silent' majority as the politicians call it. If we put it like this, it follows that they go about their lives largely unseen, unheard, and unsung—yet they comprise the vast mass of adolescents occupying what I am purposefully calling in this chapter the 'middleground'. By definition, they are the ones who find themselves more or less at home with the system in all its aspects—social, political, economic, etc; the ones who seem to adapt most readily and easily to the 'necessities' of life, as we the 'realistic' older generation see them. Above all, this means that they are in tune with the technology (as Erikson would put it) of our present age. Whether it be a flair for salesmanship, repairing television sets, or programming a computer, they quickly find they have something to offer which society wants, and hence offers them, in return, a suitable niche in its workforce, a place in the socio-economic hierarchy. Indeed, the adolescents we are now talking about very quickly tend to marry and become small family units ready to move around the country from one estate to the next—exactly the kind of efficient working unit which the economic organisation of our society demands. A reciprocal relationship is very quickly built up in which society finds its values confirmed and justified in the life of such a young couple, and they correspondingly find a secure 'positive' identity through the economic contribution they make in the adult world.

Erikson makes the same point in speaking of such adolescents *becoming* what they *do*, and of the process of 'cultural consolidation' which thereby takes place. Because they fit into the technology of the age, they also come to accept the value system that goes with it. Thus they respond readily to the blandishments and invitations issued by the advertising arm of that technology: from eight-track stereo in the latest modified version of the family car, through central heating, colour television, and double glazing in their homes, to holidays in exotic islands abroad via supersonic airliners. Whether our society can continue indefinitely with a value system which is based squarely and simply on the economic facts of life is another matter. For a long time, material advancement (or as we prefer to call it economic 'progress' and a 'higher standard of living') has seemed to be the only goal towards which we strive for most of our lives. And it is no coincidence that those who have begun to question the value system which seems to be implicit in any advanced industrialized society have concerned themselves with a multitude of ecological issues, and speak of the 'quality' of the environment, and hence the 'quality' of life for those who have to live in it.

In striking contrast to those adolescents who very readily come to accept the majority's version of reality are those whom society shows very little hesitation in condemning to a 'negative' identity at a comparatively early age—the so-called 'juvenile delinquents'. As a result of all the work done in this area in recent years it is becoming increasingly clear that the vast majority of these adolescents have suffered from very severe maternal deprivation in early childhood, severe enough at any rate to have led them to develop a fundamental mistrust of the world in the sense of a feeling that there is no one around upon whom they can rely to provide love, security, and affection; and that anything they are going to get in this world they have to get for themselves, if necessary by force. In the worst cases, of course, the anger and fury at having nothing, as they feel it, leads in adolescence to destructive behaviour which seems to carry the implicit message, 'We'll make sure you have nothing too', i.e. vandalism, physical assault, and all the other acts of sense-

176

less violence which regularly hit the headlines. The grossly over-simplified version of reality which underlies such behaviour has been expressed by some researchers as the 'Them-Us' syndrome. Such a state of mind can again be seen as a version of the basic good-bad dichotomy operating in the very early stages of life; and hence as an indication that, with the true delinquent, things do indeed go wrong from the very outset. I say 'true' because, as always, those who feel responsible for the emerging delinquent fervently hope and pray that his behaviour is a passing 'phase', the exploration of a violent acting out extreme from which he will eventually retreat into the middleground. But for the adolescent who has truly split his world into 'those who are on my side' and 'those who are against me', the passing of time merely reinforces these extremes, and thus serves to confirm his distorted view of reality. And of course, those who *are* only too eager to confirm him in his 'negative' identity provide experiences on which, as Erikson points out, the identity itself feeds and rigidifies. Ultimately the point is reached where society bestows the final seal of negative approval in branding him a 'delinquent'—and if the behaviour continues, a 'criminal'.

The typical life history of such a negative identity needs no elaboration here. But I should like also to mention the perhaps more disturbing (because more incomprehensible) example of the radical student, quite able to express his political views in a highly intelligent and articulate fashion (indeed one might almost say a 'natural' politician), who nonetheless also resorts to direct action (sit-ins and protest marches, even bombings and kidnappings), apparently in the belief that this is the only way in which society can ever be changed, i.e. come to share his version of reality. In this case there is even less justification on the face of it for a view of the world which has been knowingly and deliberately over-simplified. Yet on the other hand, we might argue that it is precisely this kind of intellectual over-simplification of reality which the academic subculture encourages—as if the belief 'Now anything is possible' were indeed a valid one, at least in the comfortable confines of one's ivory tower, and

177

the safe world of one's head. The radical student might well argue that to stay the intellectual locked in the realm of ideas and concepts is precisely the identity which society would like him to accept. We should also bear in mind that a great many students come from safe and secure middle-class backgrounds (sometimes made so at the expense of extremes of devotion in their parents' lives) which have protected them from the harsher and more painful aspects of the world at large.

The need to challenge this safe, secure, and at the same time remote and intellectual version of reality leads many students to stage a kind of confrontation with the hardest and harshest realities the world has to offer—whether it be trying to get to India on £30, or trying to live as a member of a self-sufficient agricultural commune. However selfish such behaviour may seem on occasions, it does at least represent an attempt on the part of the adolescent to experience for himself some of the more concrete and practical aspects to reality, and has much of the flavour of playful experimentation to it. But where the ideological commitment has already become strong and deep-rooted, the confrontation may well consist of direct action of an altogether different kind: the attempt to *impose* an ideal version of reality on a world which, unfortunately for the idealist, shows little sign of changing as quickly as he might wish. The resulting frustration, of course, only leads to further extremes of behaviour, the 'negative' and 'destructive' aspects of which, as always, figure prominently in the mass media.

But the dividing line between what society praises as a 'constructive' contribution to its way of life and condemns as a 'destructive' attack on its very existence is often pitifully thin—which is as it should be if what we are really talking about is whose version of reality we choose to accept. For example, because of the severe shortage of houses in England, and the resulting overcrowding, and in many cases homelessness, some people 'took the law into their own hands', and occupied any empty houses they could find (often ones which the local council had bought prior to their being demolished). Such people were called 'squatters', dealt with by bailiffs or in the courts, and initially showed every sign of becoming one of society's more popular 'negative' sideshows. But as time went on, and the more eloquent squatters pleaded their case in the media, it became apparent that it was a very sound one, that there was no valid reason why homeless families should not be allowed to occupy empty houses which might not be demolished for five years or more. In the end, several local councils reached an agreement with what were now called 'Squatters Associations', and the squatters themselves began to be seen as having rightfully brought into public focus a national problem which the Government 'should do something about'. In other words, they were well on the way towards assuming 'positive' identities in the eyes of society.

Countercultures

Many such movements as the above, political or otherwise, arise during the life of any society. They suggest a change in the way that society organises and runs itself. They put forward for consideration a different version of reality; they propose in essence a change in the value system on which that society is based. When any such movement begins to make headway in society at large, it begins to assume the status of what we might call a counterculture. One of the clearest examples of such movements to date was the Vietnam peace movement which started shakily on the campuses of American colleges; reached its peak perhaps at the 1968 Democratic Convention in Chicago (when it was made brutally clear whose version of reality was to be accepted); and only, some four years later, appears to have had some effect on those who run by far the most powerful (if our value system is based on gross national product) country in the world. From a cynical viewpoint, of course, we might argue that this movement was motivated not by any ideological commitment, but by pure self-interest: the simple wish not to die in a paddy field 6,000 miles from home. But the birth of the movement was motivated as much as anything, I think, by counteraction against the value system

179

implicit in depersonalising any materialistic, advanced industrialised society.

I have mentioned the ecological issue because it brings up a very important point about the idealism of youth, namely whether the elder generation (the Establishment if you like) is at all comprehending, let alone sympathetic, to what is being said. In this case (perhaps again out of self-interest, since it is often their homes and 'quality of life' that are being threatened as well) the parents of those adolescents who are most vociferous in their condemnation of the pollution they see all around them have been very quick to jump on the ecological bandwagon. Indeed in England, 'respectable' Sunday newspapers now organise surveys and run competitions for children in which the task is to measure and record the pollution in their particular area or neighbourhood. In other words, the idealism of youth has *not* been met with, at best, exasperated shrugs of the shoulders and vague mutterings about being 'unrealistic'; at worst, with scornful and contemptuous sneering, and accusations of being 'irresponsible' etc. Therefore the idealistic adolescent does not feel driven into a vicious circle of frustration, leading to more extreme behaviour on his part, in the attempt to force the issue upon the attention of his elders—followed inevitably by further repression and condemnation from their side. We might almost define the totalitarian nature of any government in terms of the degree of resistance it puts up to any change in the value system by which it governs the country.

This leads us back to the paradox about adolescents that I mentioned at the beginning of this chapter. On the one hand, the more we allow ourselves to become angrily preoccupied with an extreme of attitude or behaviour in an adolescent, the more likely we are to ensure its continuation. Yet at the same time, if we are not prepared to call a halt somewhere along the line then, almost always, the adolescent feels obliged to escalate the process one stage further in his desperate need to establish that there are indeed limits to his behaviour which society is prepared to set. Or, to put it another way, that society is willing to help him contain the tremendous anxiety that goes along with the belief, 'Now *anything* is possible.' It is indeed crucial that the elder generation never abandon what Erikson calls 'their vital role as sanctioneers and critics' and always be prepared to state loudly and clearly the nature of the value system on which they have based their lives. And if, at the same time, we, the tired realists, can pause for a moment to consider the kernel of truth or validity that *may* lie behind the extreme view which the adolescent is propounding, then the way is open for him to retreat and meet us in the middleground—and just maybe to collaborate with us in bringing about together a change in the version of reality which is accepted by the majority.

It is in this frame of mind, I think, that we should approach what is now being increasingly called in the media the 'alternative society'. This 'counterculture' represents a fusion of a large number of adolescent subcultures, all of which in some way seem to feel out of step with the value system of the larger society. Many of its members are 'drop-outs', i.e. they cannot accept the path to a 'successful' job or career which often seems already mapped out for them by society; many are members of the drug subculture, i.e. they do not get their pleasure and relaxation from the same drugs (and usually the same leisure activities) as the rest of society; some have difficulty reconciling their sexual identities with the norms prevailing at large, others their political beliefs. What distinguishes them from countless other adolescent groups and subcultures through the ages, in my view, is the fact that they understand the power of the various means of communication available in modern society, and make full use of them. At a straightforward level this, of course, serves to swell their numbers; but more importantly, they show no hesitation in using the media to propose an alternative to the value system on which they see society at present being based.

A great many of their newspapers, magazines, and periodicals do, of course, contain the kind of anti-authoritarian statements which are more or less *de rigueur* in any adolescent subculture; and it would be easy to succumb to

181

the temptation of writing them off as 'left-wing scum' (choose the political epithet you apply for those who have no grasp of your version of reality). This, I think, is a dangerous oversimplification; but, at the risk of being accused of offering another one, I would like to suggest that the value system which underlies much of their communications represents a sincere attempt to modify the traditional puritan virtues on which much of any advanced industrialised society is based, and to replace these virtues with an ethic which is based less on self-help than on helping others, less on self-interest than the welfare of all; above all, less on self-projection than on self-exploration. It may seem that, in an underhand way, I am talking about conservative as opposed to socialist attitudes. But if we can keep away from the extremes, political or otherwise, the grain of truth in what the alternative society proposes is, in my view, something very much to do with exposing the myths of economic 'progress' and a 'higher standard of living'.

From this standpoint, I think, we may be in a better position to understand much of the behaviour of the so-called 'alternative' society. It should not surprise us that many of its members have no qualms about taking money from the Welfare State, and are quite prepared to 'rip off' whatever material wealth they find lying around. It should not surprise us that many of them turn their backs on the cities and urban life, and choose to eke out an existence at a bare subsistence level in countries such as India where the economy is based largely upon agriculture. Indeed, it should not really surprise us that some of them go to the lengths of trying to set up agricultural communes which are self-sufficient in order to escape from the industrial rat-race. In a very broad sense, there is an attempt to return to 'Nature', whether it be expressed in current fads for health foods, abhorrence of pesticides and battery rearing of farm animals, or hatred for the concrete jungle and its polluted atmosphere of exhaust fumes. The implicit message in all such behaviour is clearly an outright rejection of the prevailing economic system and organisation of Western society.

In a very important sense, their communes represent a real

challenge to the notion of the small and essentially isolated family unit in its neat house on a new estate, waiting to be told by the glossy magazines what it wants next. Again, the overriding wish seems to be to stand outside the economic system as much as possible.

This brings us to the interesting situation of 'straight' society pandering to the alternative society. For it is of course true that, as with the record industry, the music of the alternative society has been just another product successfully sold, indeed convincingly oversold, to the teenage market according to the usual methods and techniques. Similarly, of course, the theatre, film, and publishing industries have no hesitation in catering for the needs of the alternative society so long as they can make money out of it. Indeed, as is well known, the big tobacco companies in the USA have already registered certain brand names in preparation for the day when the smoking of cannabis is declared no longer illegal. I think what this illustrates is simply that it is extremely difficult, if not impossible, to go against the economic system of the society in which one lives when it is geared so exclusively to the satisfaction of consumer needs. Unless, of course, you nationalise the means of production, and then, like all the best dictatorships, are in a position to impose your own value system, regardless of the consideration of others. Perhaps what this brings out most clearly is that, as always, a clash of value systems must result in a compromise, one side giving way in some areas, the other in others.

One of the areas in which the alternative society has stood its ground so far is its emphasis on self-knowledge and self-exploration, whether this be achieved through 'consciousness expanding' (hallucinogenic) drugs, yoga, and meditation; or 'rapping sessions', communal living, and encounter groups. I think this stands very much in contrast to what I earlier called self-projection, i.e. the creation of a good 'image' via material wealth and success, possession of the latest status symbols—in short, where the emphasis is entirely on external appearances rather than internal reality. It is no coincidence that the 'straight' majority uses drugs in an almost pathetic attempt to get rid of the stresses and strains that are the inevitable concomitant of life in an advanced industrialised society. Whether it is beer for the worker on the assembly line, a 'highball' for the high-powered executive, or sleeping tablets for his housebound wife, the aim is the same—to forget.

As always, there is a countercharge, that the so-called self-exploration is really pure selfishness, an escapist retreat into a mindless and irrelevant self-absorption and self-preoccupation, a refusal to face the grim reality of the problems facing the world today. But I believe, on the contrary, that the alternative society, so far from shirking any of these issues, is, through the life styles its members adopt, *suggesting some sort of change* in the value system which is inherent in any advanced industrialised society. What is important is that we do not get preoccupied with the extremes of attitude or behaviour manifested by the alternative society; *nor* fail to show them that we too have a value system, and are not going to abandon it overnight. We should not take adolescents too seriously, either by wholeheartedly embracing what they have to offer, or by condemning it outright. But unless society is prepared to lend a tolerant quarter of an ear to its wilder elements—whether they be 'adolescents', 'prophets', 'madmen', or sometimes even 'scientists'—it will assuredly never change—for 'better' or for 'worse'. I cannot help feeling it is the misfortune of adolescents that, in the modern world, it is their destiny always to be seen as the barbarian hordes who threaten civilisation itself.

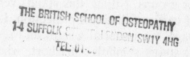

Index

Index